AGILE
IN PLAIN
SIGHT

You've Been Agile All Along
You Just Didn't Know It

ALIU W. ADEWALE

LANIKELL GLOBAL

First published in the United States, 2025 by Lanikell
Global

A CIP catalogue record for this book is available from the
British Library

ISBN: 979-8-218-87379-0

Typeset in Great Britain by Moonbeam Books UK,
Ascot, Berkshire, United Kingdom.

Lanikell Global Publishers
3631 Truxel Road, #1236, Sacramento, California, 95834

Disclaimer

Every story in this book is drawn from real-life experiences - whether from my workplace, social interactions, or personal journey. To respect privacy, I have changed some names and identifying details, but the lessons remain entirely authentic.

Contents

Foreword

When I first met Adewale, I could see right away that he had a natural instinct for problem-solving, collaboration, and adaptability – three essential pillars of Agile. He wasn't just interested in understanding Agile as a framework; he wanted to embrace it as a mindset. Watching his journey from learning and applying Agile to now teaching it through this book has been incredibly rewarding.

Agile is more than just a methodology. It's a way of thinking, a philosophy that values people, interactions, and continuous improvement. And what makes *Agile In Plain Sight* truly special is that it doesn't just explain Agile – it brings it to life. Through engaging storytelling, real-world scenarios, and practical lessons, Adewale has crafted a book that demystifies Agile for anyone, whether you're a newcomer or a seasoned professional.

One of the most important lessons in Agile is that the best learning doesn't come from rigid processes or textbooks – it comes from experience. It comes from making mistakes, iterating, and improving. That's exactly what this book offers: a practical, experience-driven guide that helps readers connect Agile principles to everyday situations. Whether it's navigating stakeholder relationships, fostering collaboration, or adapting to change, *Agile in Plain Sight* provides a roadmap to success.

As someone who has coached and mentored countless professionals in Agile, I can say with confidence that this book is a must-read. It strips away complexity and focuses on what really matters: applying Agile in a way that makes a tangible impact. If you're ready to not just understand Agile but *live* it, you're holding the right book in your hands.

Enjoy the journey.

Lanre Dabiri (eLDee)
Agile Coach, Real Estate Developer

Introduction

Agile is everywhere. Whether we realize it or not, many of us have been living by its principles long before we even knew what Agile was. We adapt, collaborate, inspect, and adjust daily – at home, at work, and in life. The challenge is recognizing these behaviors and intentionally applying them in a professional Agile environment. That's where this book comes in.

At its core, Agile is a mindset – one built on four values and twelve guiding principles. It is not just a methodology or framework; it's a way of thinking and working that prioritizes adaptability, collaboration, and customer satisfaction. While frameworks like Scrum, Kanban, or Scaled Agile Framework (SAFe) provide structure, true agility comes from how we think and respond to change.

One of my mentors, Lanre Dabiri (eLDee), an experienced Agile coach, once shared an analogy that shaped my understanding of Agile. He compared its twelve principles to the Ten Commandments – not in a religious sense, but as guiding principles that shape behavior. Just as the Ten Commandments include principles such as *"Honor your father and mother," "You shall not steal," and "You shall not kill"*, Agile has its own twelve principles. Following these principles can make our work easier in a project environment, just as adhering to ethical and moral guidelines can help us navigate life more harmoniously.

I want to be clear – As a person of faith, I approach this comparison with profound respect for all beliefs. This powerful analogy provided a monumental shift in my understanding of Agile. It served as the crucial lens, connecting Agile theory to my own personal experiences. In many ways, I realized I had already been practicing Agile principles in my daily life before I even knew what Agile was.

I've done a lot of things in my career, but discovering and embracing Agile has been one of my biggest wins. I see myself as an agent of change – someone who believes in continuous learning, adaptation, and growth. Transitioning into an Agile role, whether as a Scrum Master, Product

Owner, or Agile Project Manager, requires more than theoretical knowledge. It demands the ability to live the principles and apply them in real-world scenarios.

The perspective presented is grounded in years of hard-won, hands-on experience as an Agile Project Manager, Scrum Master, Release Train Engineer (RTE) and Agile Coach, working directly with real teams to overcome real-world challenges. This book is the definitive resource on the Agile mindset in action, moving far beyond the mere memorization of frameworks. I translate high-level Agile principles into tangible, real-life scenarios. We'll discover how Agile principles can be applied in everyday situations, both inside and outside the workplace.

This book is for newcomers who want to succeed in Agile environments, professionals pivoting into Agile roles, and even seasoned practitioners seeking fresh, practical insights. It is also for anyone simply curious to see how the values in Agile and its principles may already be showing up in their day-to-day life – often without realizing it.

The stories shared in this book bridge Agile principles with the realities of everyday life, each carrying a meaningful lesson. My hope is that they spark your own reflections and inspire you to apply Agile principles with more clarity and intention.

Agile is already in front of us. Let's explore Agile in Plain Sight together.

Chapter 1

Oga Number One: The Power of Making People Feel Number One

Growing up in Ibadan, Oyo State, Nigeria, I often found myself at the bustling workshop of my dad's friend, known to everyone as "Oga Number One". "Oga" is a popular slang term in Nigeria, originally from the Yoruba tribe, meaning "master" or "boss." It's widely used to show respect – whether for someone in a high position, a senior colleague, or even casually among friends. And Number One? That needs no introduction. It's the absolute best.

So, calling someone Oga Number One isn't just giving them a title – it's like putting a crown on their head and rolling out the red carpet, a title fit for royalty. And truly, Oga Number One wore it well. And if you're wondering, yes, Nigerians love their grand gestures. Where else can someone get a standing ovation just for being the neighborhood mechanic?

Oga Number One's garage was always alive with the clatter of wrenches, the rhythmic hum of engines, and the occasional burst of laughter from customers waiting under a faded awning, shaded from the relentless Nigerian sun. The crackling of a battered radio playing Afrobeat tunes added a nostalgic rhythm to the atmosphere. The air hung heavy with the heat of the sun, mingling with the pungent smells of grease, petrol, and roasted plantains from a nearby vendor. Customers chatted and joked under the shade, their voices blending with the lively banter of apprentices at work. Despite the chaos, everything moved with purpose, guided by his steady hand.

More than just a mechanic, Oga Number One was a cornerstone of the community. Nearly 75% of the town's commercial vehicles found their way to his garage, drawn by his unmatched reputation. He stood tall and broad-shouldered, his faded blue jumpsuit marked with oil stains from countless repairs which was a testament to his skill and dedication. His weathered hands moved with practiced precision, and a pair of safety goggles hung loosely around his neck. His sharp eyes missed nothing, constantly scanning the workshop to ensure every detail was perfect. With a crooked smile and a calm, deep voice, he carried an air of quiet authority that put both customers and apprentices at ease.

Despite the respect he commanded, not every interaction was pleasant. Some customers, frustrated by delays or the stress of running their businesses, would storm into the workshop shouting and demanding unrealistic repair timelines.

"I need this car ready by tomorrow morning!" they'd yell.

Their voices echoing above the noise of the garage. Others would criticize his work without fully understanding the complexities of the issues at hand. It wasn't uncommon to see a customer wagging a finger in his face or raising their voice, convinced that their demands should take precedence over the other vehicles waiting for his attention.

Yet, no matter how rude or impatient they were, he never lost his temper. Instead, he would listen intently, nodding as if their complaints were the most reasonable requests in the world, his calm demeanor diffusing even the most heated situations.

Curious about his unshakeable calm, I once asked him why he always responded with patience, never raising his voice or showing frustration.

"Oga, how do you do it?" I asked one afternoon, leaning against a dusty car hood in his workshop.

"How come you never lose your temper, even when customers are shouting or making impossible demands?"

He chuckled, wiping his oil-streaked hands on an old rag.

"Ah, Adewale, you young people are always in a hurry to shout or fight," he said, shaking his head.

"Do you know why they call me Oga Number One?"

I raised an eyebrow. *"Because you're the best mechanic in town?"*

He laughed, a deep, hearty sound that echoed across the garage. "Not just that, my boy. It's because I understand one thing very well…"

"If you argue with a customer, you'll lose twice."

I frowned, puzzled. *"Twice? What do you mean?"*

He leaned in slightly, his expression serious yet kind. "You see, if you argue with a customer, the first thing you lose is their respect. Nobody wants to work with someone who makes them feel small or unheard.

The second thing you lose is their business. Even if you're the best mechanic, they'll walk away and never come back. And when they leave, they take ten potential customers with them."

I nodded slowly, beginning to grasp the weight of his words. He continued, his voice steady and filled with conviction. "But when you listen… truly listen… they feel valued. Even if they are wrong, they will leave with their dignity intact. And that dignity is the bridge that keeps them coming back."

The simplicity of his wisdom struck me like a hammer to an anvil. It wasn't just about fixing cars; it was about fixing relationships, nurturing trust, and creating loyalty.

"*So, patience is the key?*" I asked, eager to understand more.

Oga Number One smiled, tapping his temple. "Patience is the foundation, my boy. But the real key is making them feel like Number One. When people feel valued, they see you differently, not just as a mechanic, but as someone they can rely on. That kind of trust builds more than a business; it builds a legacy."

I stood there in awe, realizing that his philosophy wasn't just about running a successful garage. It was a blueprint for life. His words resonated deeply, planting seeds of understanding that would later bloom as I embraced Agile principles. The wisdom of Oga Number One wasn't confined to a workshop; it was universal, a timeless reminder that relationships and respect are the true engines of success. I realized that he had been practicing its principles long before I knew their name. And it wasn't only in his patience that this showed. He also had a way of proving progress early, a habit that resonates deeply with the call for early delivery of Agile.

In many ways, Oga Number One also practiced "early delivery" without calling it that. He rarely left customers in the dark. Even if a repair was going to take days, he would often show small signs of progress – tightening a loose bolt, getting the engine to at least sputter, or explaining what he had already diagnosed. These small updates reassured customers that value was already being delivered, even before the car was fully repaired. That glimpse of progress built confidence and trust, turning waiting time into an experience of involvement rather than frustration.

What I didn't know then was that I was already witnessing the essence of Agile. It would take years and a journey into project management for me to recognize that Oga Number One's philosophy was Agile in action and how his wisdom was quietly shaping the way I approached people, projects, and leadership.

Years later, as I explored the world of Agile, I realized that Oga Number One had been practicing its principles long before I knew their name. His approach to valuing people and fostering trust wasn't just good business; it planted the seeds of a mindset centered on customer satisfaction.

It was the embodiment the first principle of Agile: Our highest priority is to satisfy the customer through the early and continuous delivery of valuable software. His philosophy also reflected two core Agile values: prioritizing "individuals and interactions over processes and tools" and "customer collaboration over contract negotiation." What I witnessed in that workshop was far more than customer service; it was a mindset built on relationships and collaboration, the true foundation of success, long before I even knew it had a name.

Through his example, I learned that Agile is not just a methodology but a mindset. An approach to life and work that values people, relationships, and adaptability. He had mastered this mindset effortlessly, without ever knowing what Agile was. Yet, the essence of Agile was right there in his workshop, in every interaction, every compromise, and every moment of unwavering patience.

As I reflect on Oga Number One's approach to his customers, I realize how much it mirrors the Agile philosophy I adopted later in my career. In the world of Agile project management, stakeholders, both internal and external, are our customers. They are at the heart of every decision, and we must put them in the driver's seat.

My mindset shifted dramatically when I embraced Agile. I began to see that empowering stakeholders wasn't just about meeting their needs but creating an environment where they felt heard, valued, and in control. When stakeholders feel like they are in the driver's seat, something remarkable happens: they start to listen, they are eager to learn, and most importantly, they feel happy. It's in this happiness and sense of ownership that collaboration thrives, and projects find their true momentum.

As an Agile Lead, I've witnessed how the same principles Oga Number One lived by – listening, patience, and collaboration – can redefine team dynamics and strengthen stakeholder trust. These values have become cornerstones of my professional approach.

In one project, I noticed a stakeholder repeatedly raising concerns during sprint reviews, feeling overlooked in the decision-making process. Instead of brushing it off, I scheduled a one-on-one session to truly listen and understand his perspective. His feedback revealed a communication gap between the development team and the business unit, which was causing frustration. By addressing this, we implemented a simple weekly update system that not only resolved the issue but also boosted stakeholder trust. This small adjustment led to a 25% increase in team velocity and a stronger partnership between teams.

Reflecting on this now, I see the seeds of this mindset planted early on in my life. Oga Number One, I saw how his calm, respectful way of treating his customers always left them satisfied, even in challenging situations. His approach reinforced the idea that relationships and trust are at the heart of any success, an idea that Agile has refined into a guiding principle.

In real projects, things rarely go exactly as planned. Deadlines can slip, scope can creep, and new requirements almost always emerge along the way. These challenges are inevitable, and no methodology, Agile or otherwise, can eliminate them completely. But what truly defines success is how we respond when they do happen. Do we treat our stakeholders as adversaries to defend against, or as partners to collaborate with? This choice determines whether they walk away frustrated or walk away feeling respected, even when things don't go perfectly.

When we engage stakeholders with transparency and collaboration, they begin to see value even before the final delivery. A delayed feature becomes less of a setback when they understand why it's happening, how their input has shaped the process, and when they feel part of the decision-making journey. That inclusion is itself value. It reassures them that their investment of time, trust, and money is being honored. And when we combine that inclusion with respectful treatment, they not only forgive the obstacles but often become champions of the team. In the long run, this is what transforms satisfied stakeholders into loyal partners who continue to collaborate with us.

Just as Oga Number One's small signs of progress built confidence in his customers, in projects early delivery works the same way. A working prototype, a demo of part of the feature, or even an early integration test can give stakeholders something tangible. These early wins allow them to see value unfolding, build trust in the process, and offer feedback when it's still cheap and easy to adjust course.

When stakeholders see this kind of early value, their perspective shifts. Delays or scope changes feel less threatening because they've already seen progress with their own eyes. Much like Oga Number One's customers who stayed patient after witnessing small fixes, stakeholders grow more confident when they experience working pieces along the way. This rhythm of steady deliveries creates momentum, reassurance, and a sense that their investment is producing results long before the final product is complete.

This principle of prioritizing stakeholder satisfaction is one I've seen succeed across all my roles, whether as a Scrum Master, Agile Project Manager, Agile Coach, or Release Train Engineer (RTE). Each capacity brought stakeholders with unique expectations, challenges, and goals. Yet, the approach remained consistent, echoing the wisdom of Oga Number One: empower them, collaborate with them, and make them feel like co-pilots in the journey. This mindset has become my navigating compass, reminding me that true success lies in building alignment, collaboration, and a shared sense of ownership.

Many of us have encountered our own "Oga Number One" in life. Someone who unknowingly embodies values we later come to admire. For me, it was through my experience with Oga Number One that I was introduced to Agile Principle #1 long before I knew its name.

His philosophy wasn't just about fixing cars. It was about building trust, fostering collaboration, and prioritizing people – the foundation of true success in both life and Agile.

Takeaway for Readers:
Our highest priority is to satisfy the customer through the early
and continuous delivery of valuable software.

Stakeholder satisfaction thrives when they feel heard, valued, and involved. By fostering collaboration and creating a sense of ownership, you build trust and alignment that drive success. Reflect on your own "Oga Number One" moments and use those lessons to strengthen your relationships and deliver meaningful results.

Remember, customer satisfaction is not a one-time achievement but a continuous commitment. Just like Oga Number One patiently earned the loyalty of his customers day after day, we too must approach our stakeholders with consistency, respect, and openness. Showing them small but steady progress, "*early delivery of value*", reassures them that their investment is paying off. Every project, every interaction, is an opportunity to show them that they matter and when people feel like "Number One," they give their best in return.

Chapter 2
Last-Minute Magic Happens When You Open the Door to Change

It was a quiet, overcast morning in Sacramento, USA, and I was set to catch an early flight. My destination? Charlotte, North Carolina (NC). I had planned a short trip and to reconnect with someone I hadn't seen in a while. I had booked my flight with Delta Airlines about two weeks earlier, the carrier I trust to get me where I need to go without drama.

But life – as it tends to – had other plans. Boarding was just 30 minutes away when an urgent call came through. A work situation needed my attention the following morning, and I could no longer take that flight. I had to make the change right on the spot. I needed to reschedule – not tomorrow, not next week – today.

I opened the Delta app, fully expecting friction. But instead of hoops and holding music, I was met with options. Delta's system offered options to move my flight to a day that suited me better. no drama. A few taps later, I had moved my departure to a later flight and even picked a better seat.

As someone who travels frequently, I was delighted by how simple the process was. It took no more than two or three minutes – less time than I would have spent just waiting on hold for a customer representative, explaining my situation, and hoping they'd make the change without a mistake. The Delta app made everything clear and smooth. No phone bill spike. No hassle. Just a few taps on my phone, and boom – done. Rescheduled, re-seated, and right back to focusing on what mattered. That kind of smooth, self-directed experience? That's what keeps customers coming back. And honestly, that's probably what keeps me coming back too (just saying).

Delta isn't alone in this. Airlines like United, American, Alaska, and Southwest have also evolved in recent years to offer same-day flight changes – often for free or a modest fee, especially for Main Cabin or higher fares. Their apps and support systems make it easier than ever for travelers to adjust plans on the fly, whether it's due to weather, work, or unexpected life events.

Not every airline gets this right. Budget carriers like Spirit and Frontier, while affordable, allegedly have a reputation for being less flexible when it comes to same-day changes, at least without extra fees or premium upgrades. And in moments of urgent need, that difference matters.

This kind of flexibility is no accident. In a highly competitive industry, these legacy carriers have learned that the real edge isn't just in having the newest aircraft or the most routes – it's in being able to adapt to customers' changing needs, even at the last minute. That's how they retain loyalty in a world full of choices.

As the customer, I realized that Delta's flexibility in handling my last-minute change was exactly what earned my trust. If that same capability didn't exist, and I knew another airline could meet my needs more easily, I wouldn't hesitate to go with them instead the next time I plan to fly. But because Delta provided that flexibility when it mattered most, it reinforced why they've become my first choice when it comes to air travel.

You're probably wondering, "What does Delta Airlines, or my trip to Charlotte NC, have to do with Agile Principle #2?"

After reading through a few paragraphs, it's a fair question. Yes, I know. But stay with me to connect the dots.

Understand this: Agile Principle #2 doesn't require a software team, a Scrum board, or rocket science. It's about adaptability. It's about creating systems, just like Delta and other airlines have, that welcome change, even at the last possible moment. The same way I was able to adjust my plans on the fly – without friction – Is the same way our Agile teams should be able to shift gears when a customer's needs evolve. Whether the change comes one week before the deadline or 30 minutes before boarding, the mindset is the same: "How can we make this work for the customer's benefit?"

In Agile terms, my travel plan was the original "requirement." But that requirement changed — suddenly and late in the process due to new information. I, the customer, now had a new requirement: to cancel my current booking and reschedule the flight for a later date and I had to make that change right on the spot, just minutes before boarding.

This is exactly what Agile Principle #2 teaches us: "Welcome changing requirements, even late in development. Agile processes harness change for the customer's competitive advantage." Change isn't the enemy. It's an opportunity. When our processes are designed to welcome changing requirements, even late in the journey, we're better positioned to serve our customers and win their loyalty.

Delta's ability to support my change, in that small but crucial moment, wasn't just about convenience. It was a strategy. It showed me that they're committed to supporting customer adaptability, not just their own internal processes. That's the very definition of competitive advantage through change – the kind Agile teams aim to deliver.

And the truth is, this kind of responsiveness isn't unique to airlines. It shows up in other areas of life too — places you might not even expect.

Agile Principle #2 might have been originally designed with software development teams in mind, but it's more than just a guideline for tech work – it's a mindset.

Let's look at it from a different angle, this time in a completely different industry – hospitality. We'll come to eventually understand how this mirrors my previous story perfectly. You'll also begin to recognize that the idea of welcoming change, even late in the process, isn't limited to airlines or software teams. It's happening right in front of us, more often than we think.

Imagine this: You've booked a standard queen room for a short stay. You arrive at the hotel lobby with your wife and young child, just hoping to check in smoothly. But before you can even ask, the front desk attendant looks at your reservation, glances at your family, and says, "Would you like a complimentary upgrade to a king room or a double queen for more space? We have availability."

In that moment, they welcomed a new requirement that emerged late in your customer journey, right at the point of check-in. You didn't originally request a bigger room, but based on context, the hotel adapted to your needs.

And if you're the one who requests the upgrade? The principle still holds. The hotel's willingness to listen and respond, quickly and helpfully, changes the tone of your stay and goes a long way in building long-term loyalty.

Now you might be thinking, "Well, why didn't you just book a bigger room from the start?"

But the truth is… plans change all the time.

What if your wife and kids weren't originally part of the travel plan? Or maybe it's a family reunion, and the idea was for them to stay with relatives while you stayed at the hotel, until the very last moment, when you realize the space your family provided is too small.

Or someone who wasn't expected, maybe an uncle or cousin, shows up at the reunion, and now you have to shuffle things around to make everyone comfortable.

These different scenarios can happen here. And the very act of thinking through those possibilities, and adjusting your plans accordingly, is a mindset in itself, one that welcomes change, even when you didn't plan for it. You're living Principle #2 perfectly without even realizing it.

Because in that moment, you're not thinking through just for yourself, you're thinking through for your family's advantage. And in this context, your family mirrors the customer. Their comfort, their experience, their needs become the priority. That's the heart of Agile Principle #2: welcoming change to serve the people who matter most.

This mirrors what happens in Agile development. Sometimes, stakeholders themselves ask for an upgrade or maybe a better user interface, an additional feature, or a workflow tweak. Other times, the development team spots an opportunity for improvement and checks in with the Product Owner (PO) or stakeholder:

"Would you be interested in this enhancement? It won't delay delivery and will improve usability."

That conversation is Agile in action, just like the hotel staff asking,

"Would you prefer a higher floor?"

"Would you like a view or a room near the elevator?"

On the development side, it sounds like:

"Will this change affect your Go-live timeline?"

"Is this a must-have or a nice-to-have for this software or application?"

Whether it's in airline, hospitality, or software, the essence is the same: Respond to change with empathy and agility.

The best Agile teams, like the best hotels, don't just accommodate change — they embrace it as a way to elevate the experience.

Speaking of great Agile teams, I once had the privilege of working with one of the best. They were so mature in their approach that I often found myself asking, "How do they make embracing change look so easy?"

Was it because of their experience?

Was it because they had the best Agile lead? (Which is me, by the way – lol.)

Was it because they were so used to demanding stakeholders?

Or maybe because most changes were small and manageable?

Nope. The real answer? It was their mindset... A mindset for change.

This team didn't just follow the Agile playbook; they embodied it. They saw change not as an interruption, but as an invitation to add value. They asked thoughtful questions, stayed solution-focused, and never treated last-minute adjustments like threats. Instead of defaulting to "We can't," their first instinct was always, "Let's explore how we might." That mindset didn't just happen overnight. it was cultivated through trust, collaboration, and a shared belief that responding to change is what makes good teams great.

One moment that vividly stands out happened during a release sprint. Go-live was under 10 days away, and I was already planning a small celebration lunch, because I'm a big believer in celebrating wins with my team, no matter how small. A win is a win, and I know from experience that recognition fuels morale and motivates people to do even more.

That morning, we had just wrapped up our daily stand-up. The rain tapped softly against the windows, and the room settled into that familiar, post-stand-up calm. Most of us were sipping coffee, reviewing the board, and easing into our work blocks. Collins, our new Product Owner, had missed the stand-up due to a scheduling conflict, he was on a stakeholder call at the same time. But just a few minutes after we closed the session, he pinged me on Teams asking if the team could wait. He had some new information to share. That's when he joined the call and unmuted his mic:

"Guys, I just got off a call with our main client. They want to change the dashboard layout… and they want it rolled out along with the other features we're launching in a few days."

Now, here's some context: Collins was filling in for Dan, our usual PO, who was out on paternity leave. Collins came from a different department and had experience working with several teams in the organization. He's a smart guy and pretty sharp. He really liked to flex that experience a bit (lol).

Before Dan went on paternity leave, he and Collins had a thorough handover. They walked through the project goals, timelines, outstanding backlog items, and upcoming stakeholder priorities. Collins had a good understanding of both the internal workings of the team and the expectations from external stakeholders, including those who were friendly and supportive, and those who were a bit more demanding or difficult to manage. He wasn't stepping in blind. In fact, he already knew me and Sharon, our Subject Matter Expert (SME), from previous cross-functional projects. So, on paper, he was well-prepared to step into the PO role.

But the moment Collins dropped that dashboard change request, we could all sense his panic. And it wasn't hard to see why. He had stepped into a demanding role mid-flight, the timeline was tight with go-live quickly approaching, and he wasn't sure if the team had the bandwidth to pull it off.

Honestly, even Stevie Wonder could've seen the panic in Collins (lol).

But here's the twist: the team didn't panic at all. They smiled, cracked a few jokes, and calmly asked Collins for more details. They wanted to understand the "Why" behind the change, the scope, and the expected outcome, just like they'd done many times before.

Collins was caught off guard. He literally asked,

"Guys... aren't you worried? Go-live is in a few days. Do you want me to tell the client we'll push this to Phase 2?"

The team said no. They told him they believed they could still accommodate the change... and they meant it.

What Collins didn't yet understand was this team didn't just "Do Agile" ... they lived it.

The teams Collins had worked with previously. They followed ceremonies. They checked boxes. But they didn't truly embrace the mindset. especially when it came to change. And so, his natural reaction to a last-minute request was panic.

But this team was different. They didn't accept every change blindly, but when they did, it was because they had asked the right questions, weighed the possibilities, and decided together that it could be done.

They quickly pulled up the updated request during refinement, broke it down into manageable tasks, and checked how it would impact the sprint backlog. A few team members volunteered to pair up and tackle the UI changes, while others adjusted testing coverage and validation flows. The team synced with Collins later that day to confirm priorities and clarify expectations. Within a few hours, the work was already in motion, not rushed, but intentional.

With just three days left before go-live, the team had completed unit testing, Quality Assurance (QA) testing, and User Acceptance Testing (UAT) without a hitch. The new dashboard changes were pushed into production alongside the original sprint scope. In the end, they delivered everything, the committed work and the last-minute stakeholder request, smooth, stable, and right on schedule.

We launched on time and held our celebration lunch as planned.

Two of our internal stakeholders joined us for the celebration lunch, Collins had personally invited them to witness the team's success firsthand. They took a moment to thank the team, not just for delivering the release, but for how professionally and calmly they handled the late-breaking change. A few external stakeholders who couldn't attend sent in messages of appreciation, calling out the team's responsiveness and reliability. It was one of those moments where you could feel that the trust between the team and its stakeholders had deepened.

During the celebration lunch, Collins pulled me aside and said, *"I love how the team responded to that change. The way they asked questions, adjusted without stress… It made my role so much easier."*

I told him, "Look, it's not that this team says yes to every change. But when they do, it's because they've dissected every angle and know how to make it happen. That's the difference."

Then I added: "Being Agile doesn't mean saying yes to everything, it means understanding when a change adds true value, and having the mindset and systems to respond without panic."

That moment helped Collins realize something big: late changes, when welcomed wisely, can actually become your competitive edge.

And in this case, it did exactly that, not just for us as a team, but for our stakeholders. By adapting quickly and delivering a better, more relevant dashboard experience before launch, we didn't just check a box, we gave our stakeholders something they could showcase confidently to their own clients and leadership. That's what Agile Principle #2 is all about. When we respond to change with clarity and purpose, we don't just stay on track, we help our customers move ahead.

As you can see, this kind of responsiveness isn't limited to flights or hotel check-ins. You've probably experienced it at a restaurant, where the chef adapts your meal when you ask for a change at the last minute. Or during a ride-share, when you switch your drop-off location mid-trip and both the app and the driver adjust without stress.

All of these are examples of Agile Principle #2 in action. It was right there, helping us adjust, adapt, and move forward, without us even knowing its name.

I bet you already have a few more examples in mind, moments in your own life when you asked for something to change at the last minute, and a person or system responded without resistance for your convenience, satisfaction, ease, or progress. These moments reflect competitive advantage in the context of Agile Principle #2. You may not have labeled it that way back then, but I bet you can now.

And do you want to know the real beauty of this principle? It's not about saying yes to chaos, it's about building enough flexibility to turn change into advantage. Whether in software, service, or everyday life, this mindset isn't just functional, it's transformative.

Takeaway for Readers:
Welcome changing requirements, even late in development. Agile processes harness change for the customer's competitive advantage.

Welcoming change isn't about embracing chaos. It's about building the mindset and systems that turn last-minute shifts into meaningful outcomes. Whether it's travel, hospitality, or software, the ability to respond without resistance creates competitive advantage and long-term trust.

Doing Agile means checking off ceremonies. Living Agile means embracing change when it matters most. This chapter proves that true agility, in teams setting or in everyday life, comes from a mindset that sees change as a path to progress, not a threat to plans.

Agile teams don't win because they avoid change. They win because they're ready for it, they welcome it, and they use it to elevate the experience and stay ahead of the curve.

Chapter 3

One Dish at a Time: Small Batches, Big Impact

If you've ever wondered what Agile really means, or need to explain it to someone, start here.

This chapter is your go-to guide. So, if someone ever asks you, 'What exactly is Agile, and where did it come from?', this chapter will walk you through the story. From the origins of traditional project management to the evolution that led to Agile, this section gives you the foundation you need to understand and explain Agile with clarity and confidence.

If I ever decided to launch a course or train people on Agile, this is exactly where I'd begin. The insights in this chapter lay the groundwork for understanding not just the 'how' of Agile, but the 'why' behind it. Before diving into frameworks, tools, or ceremonies, it's important to grasp the journey that led us here, starting with Waterfall and ending with the mindset shift that birthed Agile.

I believe that anyone reading this chapter who's already familiar with Agile has likely come across Agile Principle #3 before – or at least heard it in passing. However, if you're just beginning your Agile journey, this chapter will build on your ideas of what Agile is supposed to be.

Regardless of which group you belong to, I'm going to hold off on diving into Agile Principle #3 for now. First, I want to take you on a brief journey through the history that gave birth to Agile. Once you understand where it all started, the principle, and everything Agile stands for will make much more sense.

So, let me take you on a ride and please… I want you to fasten your seatbelt (lol).

Let's start from the beginning, long before Agile became a buzzword in boardrooms and tech teams. Before there was Agile, there was Waterfall. This was the dominant method used to manage projects, especially in engineering, manufacturing, and the early days of software development.

The Waterfall model was first formally introduced in 1970 by Dr. Winston W. Royce, who described it in a paper titled "Managing the Development of Large Software Systems." Ironically, while many later interpreted his paper as a promotion of Waterfall, Dr. Royce actually used it to highlight the model's limitations and suggest improvements.

The idea behind Waterfall was simple and logical: workflows in a straight line from one phase to the next, like water cascading down a set of steps. You start by gathering all the requirements. Then you move to design, then development, then testing, and finally deployment. Each phase must be completed before the next begins. No going back.

In certain industries like construction, aerospace, or defense, where blueprints must be precise and changes can be costly, this sequential approach made perfect sense. It brought structure, predictability, and accountability. And even today, Waterfall is still used successfully in projects where the scope is fixed and well understood from the start.

To help you picture it, imagine using an old-school Canon AE-1, one of those classic 35mm film cameras with manual focus and that satisfying shutter click. You take a series of pictures during an event, say, a birthday party. You're focused, adjusting your lens, clicking away. But here's the catch: you can't review the photos immediately. There's no screen to check for lighting, blurriness, or someone blinking in the background. You don't get to see the results until the film is fully developed, which could take days. And if something went wrong, bad lighting, closed eyes, or a finger over the lens, you won't know until it's too late. The moment is gone, and there's no going back to fix it.

That's what working in Waterfall can feel like. You gather all the requirements, plan the whole project, execute it in phases and only in the final stages do you see the "developed photo," or finished product. If expectations were misunderstood early on, you won't know until the end and by then, it may be too late or too costly to correct.

Or think about prepping an entire week's meals based on a fixed menu. You spend hours on Sunday evening cooking all your breakfasts, lunches, and dinners for the next seven days. You portion everything out in containers and stack them neatly in the fridge. It feels organized and efficient, until life happens.

Maybe you get sick of eating the same thing by Wednesday. Or you're invited out for dinner and now some meals go uneaten. Maybe you discover halfway through the week that your child no longer likes what you prepped, or your work schedule changes and you can't reheat certain meals on time. The plan was fixed, but your needs evolved… and now you're stuck with meals you no longer want, need, or enjoy.

That's how Waterfall works. You plan everything in advance with the best of intentions, but if anything changes along the way, your ability to adjust is limited. And often, you don't realize a dish didn't work, or in software terms, a feature didn't land... until it's too late to fix it easily.

In both of these examples of film photography and weekly meal prepping, the problem isn't the process itself. It's that... the process assumes everything will go perfectly the first time and that nothing will change along the way.

But in reality, preferences shift, schedules change, and unexpected needs arise. When this kind of rigid, pre-planned approach is applied to areas like software development, where customer expectations and technology evolve rapidly, it becomes risky and often inefficient.

Which brings us back to how software was made during the Waterfall era. Projects moved through a series of clearly defined stages starting from requirements gathering and ending with maintenance. Each phase had to be completed before the next one could begin. You couldn't go back to the design phase once development had started. You couldn't rethink the requirements once testing revealed a gap. Everything depended on getting it right from the start.

And even if you did need to go back and make a change, for instance a new requirement surfaced or something critical was missed, the process didn't make that easy. You still had to follow the same sequential steps, often restarting from the beginning. That meant updating the documentation, revisiting the design, and redoing development all before it could be tested and delivered again. In many cases, this wasn't just time-consuming; it was demoralizing for teams and costly for stakeholders. Change was seen as a disruption not an opportunity. And in a world that doesn't stand still, that kind of rigidity quickly became a liability.

Just to be clear, this isn't an attack on the Waterfall model. This model has served nations for many years and there are still professionals and industries that use it effectively today, and that's because the type of work they do demands it. For example, building a bridge, designing an aircraft, producing pharmaceuticals, or developing hardware. These are areas where the cost of change is extremely high, and the sequence of work must be tightly controlled. In such cases, Waterfall brings the clarity and structure needed to manage risk and meet strict regulatory standards.

But when it comes to software development, the story is different. Change is constant, feedback loops are critical, and customer needs evolve faster than documentation can keep up. The same structure that offers strength in fixed environments often becomes a weakness in dynamic ones. That's why, over time, its limitations became harder to ignore.

As technology evolved and the pace of change accelerated, the cracks in the Waterfall approach started to show, especially in software development.

One of the biggest challenges was inflexibility. Because all requirements had to be gathered upfront, there was little room to adapt when customer needs changed mid-project, which as we now know, happens more often than not. By the time a product is finally delivered, the market might have shifted, the users' needs could have evolved, or worse… the product might no longer be relevant.

Another issue was delayed feedback. In Waterfall, you might spend months designing and building before the customer even saw a working version. That meant bug, misunderstandings, or missed expectations often surfaced late – making it expensive and stressful to fix them.

Team communication also tended to be siloed. Developers did their part, testers did theirs, and customers were mostly on the outside looking in. The result? Projects often ended in frustration, blame, or a product that didn't quite hit the mark.

The industry began to realize that in fast-moving environments, we needed a different way, a model that welcomed change, delivered value early and often, and kept people – not just processes – at the center of the work.

And that's when Agile entered the story.

Agile didn't appear out of thin air. It was a response, a direct answer to the frustrations people were feeling across the industry. The desire to build better products, respond to change faster, and work more collaboratively brought together a group of seasoned practitioners who were tired of seeing projects fail under the weight of rigid plans.

In February 2001, seventeen software developers met at a ski lodge in Snowbird, Utah. These weren't just coders, they were thought leaders and innovators from different backgrounds who had experimented with lighter, more adaptive ways of working.

Together, they drafted what is now known as the Agile Manifesto, a brief but powerful document that captured the heart of a new approach to working and thinking. It wasn't a framework, a certification, or a tool. It was a mindset shift.

The Manifesto begins with four core values:

Individuals and interactions over processes and tools

Working software over comprehensive documentation

Customer collaboration over contract negotiation

Responding to change over following a plan

These weren't saying the items on the right had no value but that the items on the left mattered more when it came to delivering real, meaningful outcomes.

Alongside these values, they outlined 12 guiding principles, the DNA of what we now call Agile. These principles emphasized things like early and continuous delivery, welcoming change, collaboration, sustainability, and reflection.

Agile wasn't created to throw away everything that came before it. It was created to build on what worked and improve what didn't especially in environments where change is constant, and value needs to be delivered frequently.

This brings us back to Agile Principle #3:
"Deliver working software frequently, from a couple of weeks to a couple of months, with a preference to the shorter timescale."

Among the twelve principles, this one stands out because it challenges one of the core habits of the Waterfall era... waiting until the very end to reveal anything that actually works. In traditional Waterfall projects, teams could spend weeks or even months moving through rigid, sequential phases from first gathering requirements to then designing followed by developing then by testing, and finally deployment. Only after all those stages were done would the customer finally see a working product.

This approach often meant that no real value was delivered until the very end of the project, and by that point, things may have changed. The customer's needs, the market, or even the technology could have shifted, making what was delivered no longer relevant.

Agile flips that model. Instead of holding back until everything is "done," Agile encourages delivering working value early and often, sometimes in just two or three weeks. It's not about rushing through development or skipping quality. It's about releasing something useful that the customer can see, touch, and react to – so that feedback can happen sooner rather than later.

This principle isn't just about speed; it's about responsiveness. When you deliver something small but functional, you open the door for faster feedback, course correction, and shared understanding. The shorter the loop between effort and outcome, the more confidence teams build and the better the product becomes.

In contrast to Waterfall's long phases and late surprises, Agile Principle #3 promotes early wins, faster learning, and continuous alignment. It reflects a mindset shift from "let's finish everything before we share it" to "let's share value early and improve as we go."

This principle gets to the heart of what makes Agile different. It's not about waiting for perfection. It's about delivering value early and consistently, so that feedback can guide improvement... not delay it.

Let's take a real-world look at how this plays out.

Amazon reportedly updates its website code every 11.7 seconds. Yes, you read that right. This statistic was shared during a 2011 industry conference and while the exact number today isn't public, there's no doubt the pace has only accelerated. Thousands of small changes are pushed live every day through automated pipelines and real-time monitoring. These aren't random experiments, they're deliberate, data-informed updates based on user behavior and customer feedback. That's Agile in action: short feedback loops, continuous delivery, and learning baked into the process.

Apple does it too, though differently. Think of how iOS is rolled out. Instead of waiting years for a single giant release, Apple delivers frequent updates: bug fixes, security patches, and new features. From iOS 16 to 16.1, 16.2, and beyond, each update brings incremental value. Users don't have to wait for a perfect version, they benefit from steady improvements over time. Again, it's Agile at scale: working software delivered frequently, not just at the end of a long roadmap.

Agile isn't a theory. it's how the best companies in the world stay relevant and responsive. Whether through rapid deployments or structured product releases, they understand that delivering working value early, and often, is how you stay competitive in a world that moves fast.

But how does Agile actually make that happen?

Agile frameworks such as Scrum enable teams to work in short, repeatable cycles. For example, in Scrum, teams operate in timeboxed iterations called sprints, typically lasting one to four weeks. Within that window, the team focuses on delivering a small but usable part of the product. This might be a feature, an enhancement, or even a backend improvement – anything that provides value and can be reviewed.

Each cycle includes planning, development, testing, and review all within that short span. Agile encourages cross-functional collaboration, where developers, testers, product owners, and sometimes even customers are involved throughout the process. This tight feedback loop helps teams adapt quickly and deliver value more often.

Another example is Kanban, a visual and flow-based Agile framework that doesn't rely on fixed-length sprints like Scrum but still supports the core idea of frequent, consistent delivery. In Kanban, work is managed on a board, often with columns like "To Do", "In Progress," and "Done" making the entire process transparent to everyone involved.

One of Kanban's most valuable practices is the Work In Progress (WIP) limit. This is a rule that restricts how many tasks can be actively worked on at any one time. It's designed to reduce context switching, prevent overload, and ensure that the team completes what they've started before taking on something new.

Now, here's where the contrast with Waterfall becomes clear: In a traditional Waterfall project, everything is planned upfront and often started in large batches. Multiple workstreams might be active simultaneously, with the expectation that they'll all come together neatly at the end. But this creates bottlenecks, late discoveries, and long wait times before anything is actually delivered. There's no built-in mechanism to say, "Hold on, this is too much at once."

In Kanban, and in Agile thinking overall, the WIP limit acts as a built-in discipline tool. It doesn't just say "work less"; it says "deliver more often by focusing on finishing, not starting." It promotes flow, reduces delay, and encourages incremental delivery. Whether it's through sprints in Scrum or WIP limits in Kanban, or any other Agile framework, the goal is the same – to keep value flowing, to shorten the distance between effort and feedback, and to create working solutions sooner.

And that's exactly what Agile Principle #3 is all about: Deliver working software frequently, from a couple of weeks to a couple of months, with a preference to the shorter timescale.

Agile is built to move with change and adapt to it not just respond to it retroactively. And Principle #3 captures that movement better than any other: progress isn't measured by how much is in motion, but by how much is truly working.

I know that for some readers who are familiar with Waterfall, the mention of Kanban might seem confusing. You may have seen Kanban boards being used in traditional projects and assumed that meant the team was "doing Agile." Not necessarily… just because certain tools overlap between Agile and Waterfall environments doesn't mean the underlying process or mindset is Agile. That distinction matters.

In fact, there are many Waterfall-style environments where teams use Kanban boards purely for visual task tracking and that's okay. For example, you might find Kanban boards being used in:

Testing teams managing defect workflows

Documentation teams tracking writing and review cycles

Support teams handling post-launch maintenance

These are legitimate uses of the Kanban board. However, they don't make the project Agile. They're simply using a visual tool to make traditional work easier to follow. It might improve visibility, but it doesn't change the delivery model. Agile is not about the tools. it's about the mindset and how work is structured to deliver value frequently.

Let's say you have a Waterfall software project that's in the testing phase. The QA team might use a Kanban board with columns like "To Do," "In Progress," "Fixed," and "Retested" to manage bugs and track progress. This helps them manage workload and spot bottlenecks.

But the project as a whole still follows a linear Waterfall process, where there's no cross-functional collaboration, no iterative feedback from customers, and no frequent delivery of working software.

Let's bring this chapter to a close, I want to take you back to the two examples I shared earlier: the film camera and the weekly meal prep. But this time, let's look at how those same situations would play out in an Agile environment. Seeing the contrast will help bring everything full circle and show exactly how Agile Principle #3 – delivering working software frequently – transforms the way value is created, received, and improved upon.

In a traditional Waterfall approach, we said that using a film camera meant taking all your photos first, without seeing the results, and then waiting until the film was developed to find out if anything went wrong. There was no feedback until the very end, and no way to course correct in the moment. Now imagine this same situation handled the Agile way. Instead of a film camera, you're using a digital camera or smartphone. You take a picture, review it instantly, and if something isn't right, you retake it right there on the spot. You're not guessing. You're delivering a "working photo" frequently, adjusting in real time based on what you see. That's Agile: shorter feedback loops, immediate validation, and continuous improvement.

Let's revisit the meal prep example. Earlier, we imagined cooking all meals for the week on Sunday based on a fixed menu, only to find out midweek that plans changed or tastes shifted. That's the Waterfall approach: plan everything up front, lock it in, and hope it holds.

Now think Agile. Instead of prepping meals for the entire week in one go, you plan just enough for the next day or two. You check in with your family: "How did you like yesterday's dinner? Want something different tomorrow?" You adjust portion sizes, try new ingredients, tweak the salt or sauce, and cook in smaller, manageable batches. You're still planning, but you're doing it in short cycles, using real-time feedback to guide what comes next.

That's Agile: frequent delivery, quick adjustments, and better alignment with real needs.

Both of these examples may seem simple, but that's exactly the point! Agile isn't about adding complexity. It's about making delivery more real, more responsive, and more relevant.

Agile Principle #3 reminds us that success doesn't come from waiting until everything is finished. It comes from delivering something that works, in a shorter time frame, with purpose, and with a mindset of continuous learning and improvement.

When we deliver frequently, we don't just move faster – we learn faster. We stay connected to the people we're building for, and we create space for feedback to shape what comes next.

Now you can see why and how Agile came into the picture—to make our work and lives easier through a mindset that embraces change, collaboration, and continuous delivery. Even in our everyday routines, like the examples I shared, we can see Agile in action.

Agile is a way of thinking that shows up in how we plan, adapt, and respond to feedback – both in projects and in life.

And I believe that reading this chapter will spark your own examples – moments in your life where you've been practicing Agile without even realizing it. Whether it's adjusting plans on the go, working in smaller steps, or seeking feedback before finishing something big.

Agile is already around you.

So, if someone ever asks you, "What is Agile?" or wants a better understanding of it, I hope you'll confidently point them to this chapter.

It's more than just a definition, it's a relatable explanation built on real stories, simple metaphors, and meaningful insights.

Takeaway for Readers:
Deliver working software frequently, from a couple of weeks to a couple of months, with a preference to the shorter timescale.

Agile Principle #3 reminds us that value doesn't have to be delayed. Whether in software or everyday life, working in smaller, faster cycles allows us to learn early, adjust quickly, and deliver meaningful results more frequently. Agile isn't about rushing – it's about reducing risk and increasing relevance through continuous delivery.

Agile isn't just for tech teams. it's already present in how we plan, cook, learn, and adapt in our daily lives. Delivering in small, usable batches helps us stay flexible and make improvements based on real-time feedback. This chapter shows how shifting from perfection to progress allows us to stay adaptable, reduce waste, and create more impact with less effort.

Because in the end, value delivered late is value at risk. Agile Principle #3 flips the old model by promoting shorter cycles and faster feedback. Don't wait for the "big finish" … start small, deliver often, and grow better with each step.

Chapter 4
Navigating Change with Collaboration

Change is the only constant in the world of Agile projects. It can come in many forms; resources, scope, management, governance, priorities, timelines, team composition, and technology. And while Agile welcomes change, it's not a call to be uninformed. It's essential to keep everyone in the loop about any change that impacts the project's success, especially our stakeholders.

This particular scenario was a perfect example of Agile Principle #4: "Business people and developers must work together daily throughout the project." Collaboration and transparency were vital in addressing the challenges I faced. This principle wasn't just a guideline – It was a reminder of the importance of open communication and teamwork to drive success.

I was working with a group of contractors on this project. The developers and the Product Owner (PO) were all contractors, while I was the only full-time employee in the Scrum team, which consisted of seven members. The majority of the team had limited Agile knowledge, except for the PO, Dave, who was a seasoned professional with a deep understanding of Agile. He consistently brought valuable insights to the table. Beyond our Scrum team, we had two full-time Subject Matter Experts (SMEs), Sarah and Khalid, who provided essential business context and kept us aligned with the organization's goals.

Recognizing the need for guidance, I knew I had to coach the team through the challenges ahead. My first priority was to conduct a working agreement workshop with them before we kicked off our sprint. During these sessions, we laid out our timeboxes, meeting times, rules, and discussed decision-making processes. These workshops had been crucial for every team I'd worked with, they provided the foundation for success from the very start.

We kicked off our sprint, a two-week cadence, and things started strong. By Sprint 3, it felt like we were already in the norming stage, as if we had skipped the storming stage altogether, with the performing stage just around the corner. Smiling, I knew we were on the right track. For readers unfamiliar with Tuckman's stages of group development, I encourage you to take a look. it'll give you some insight into why I was smiling. And if you're already familiar, I'm sure you're smiling too (lol).

As I mentioned, the project was still in its early phases. Everything seemed to be progressing well as we entered Sprint 4, and I was excited about how my new team and I had found our rhythm. Little did I know… the unexpected winds of change were about to blow in.

It was around 12:30 p.m., and we had just wrapped up back-to-back meetings about 30 minutes earlier, a retrospective and the sprint planning session for Sprint 4. Knowing I needed a break, I decided it was the perfect time for lunch. Sitting at my dining table, I savored a plate of jollof rice and fried chicken prepared by my favorite Nigerian takeout restaurant. The rich aroma of spices filled the air, a nostalgic reminder of my time at Oga's Number One's workshop. For those unfamiliar, jollof rice is a West African dish made with rice cooked in a flavorful tomato-based sauce with spices. It's a dish that sparks passionate debates, particularly between Nigerians and Ghanaians, over who makes it best. Historically, jollof rice is said to have originated from the Senegambian region, yet both Nigeria and Ghana have made it their own. And as a proud Nigerian, I can confidently declare that Nigerian jollof rice reigns supreme… no arguments, just saying! (lol).

As I finished my meal, the familiar chime of a Microsoft Outlook notification broke through my focus. It could only mean one of two things: an email or a meeting invite. From where I sat, about 15 feet away from my desk, the notification wasn't clear. I leaned forward, balancing my plate, but still couldn't make it out. Standing up, plate in hand, I moved closer to my desk to investigate. It was a meeting invite from Gaby, one of our stakeholders, who also managed organizational resources and had been instrumental in hiring the team. The subject line read: "Team Transition" followed by the project name. My heart sank even before opening the invite. I had a feeling this wasn't going to be good news.

Here's Gaby's meeting invite message:

"Hi Team,

I hope you're all doing well. As part of our organizational strategy, we will be transitioning the current contractor team to a full-time internal team. The primary reason for this change is sustainability. The company prefers to build long-term stability by having a dedicated, full-time team manage this project. Additionally, the internal team we are transitioning to has prior experience working on a similar application, making them well-equipped to handle the project more efficiently.

The timeline for this transition is set for two weeks, as we do not plan to renew the contractor contracts beyond that period. We appreciate the efforts of the current team and will ensure that the transition is as smooth as possible. We'll discuss more during the meeting and address any questions you may have.

Best regards,

Gaby"

I accepted the meeting invite and immediately began drafting a knowledge transfer and transition plan. The transition would involve five team members: two backend developers, one User Interface (UI)/User Experience (UX) designer, and two Quality Assurance (QA) engineers. With a tight two-week timeline, time was of the essence. My first focus was outlining a clear, phased approach for knowledge sharing so that the incoming full-time team could quickly get up to speed without disrupting the project's momentum.

While drafting the plan, I outlined the potential impact of this change on our current deliverables and sprint goals. Since the meeting invite was only extended to Gaby, Sarah, and Khalid, I planned to present my initial thoughts and concerns to them, ensuring we had a shared strategy before communicating with the rest of the stakeholders.

On the day of the meeting, I felt prepared. It was around 10 a.m., and I sat at my home office desk with a steaming cup of hot chocolate in hand. The rich aroma of cocoa filled the room, offering a brief moment of comfort before the unknowns of the discussion. I wasn't entirely sure what to expect from Gaby, Sarah, and Khalid or what their proposed transition approach would look like. I could only hope that we would find alignment on a strategy that would set the incoming team up for success while ensuring the outgoing team felt valued and appreciated for their hard work.

As I joined the virtual meeting, Gaby, Sarah, and Khalid's faces appeared one by one on the screen, each in their own remote setting. The soft hum of my laptop blended with the distant chirping of birds outside my window, adding a quiet backdrop to the unfolding conversation. The room felt still, as if everyone was quietly preparing for the big discussion. We were about to dive into a discussion that would shape the upcoming transition, and I took a deep breath, ready to navigate whatever lay ahead.

Gaby started the meeting with a brief summary of what he had written in the meeting invite. *"I know this transition might come as a surprise to some of you,"* he said, glancing at the screen. *"But we believe this change is necessary for long-term sustainability."* After outlining the key points, he paused and added, *"I'd like to open the floor now. If anyone has questions or concerns, please feel free to speak up."*

Sarah was the first to unmute. Her expression reflected a mix of concern and frustration. *"Gaby,"* she began, her tone firm but measured, *"do we know which team is going to replace the current contractors? Have they worked on similar projects for us before? I've spent a lot of time helping this team get up to speed, and I need to know if the new team has the skills and context to take over seamlessly."*

Gaby nodded, acknowledging her concerns. *"That's a valid question, Sarah. The new team has worked on a similar application for another department, and their feedback has been positive. They bring strong technical expertise and a deep understanding of our organizational processes."*

Sarah's eyes narrowed slightly as she leaned forward. *"That's reassuring to hear, but I'd still like to evaluate their experience personally. As an SME, I need to ensure they're a good fit for what we're building."*

Before Gaby could respond, Khalid spoke up, his tone cautious. *"I understand the need for sustainability, but I'm worried about the two-week* timeline. It's incredibly tight for a transition of this scale. How do we ensure the new team is set up for success without derailing our current deliverables?"

Gaby took a deep breath. *"You're right, Khalid. The timeline is aggressive, but we've outlined a phased knowledge transfer plan. The current team will document their workflows and walk the new team through the application. Adewale,"* he said, turning toward me, *"do you have any additional thoughts or concerns?"*

I unmuted, my mind racing with how to frame my input constructively. "Thanks, Gaby," I began. "I've already started drafting a transition plan focusing on knowledge transfer, but I do share Khalid's concern about the timeline. We'll need to be deliberate in prioritizing what the new team needs to know versus what can be deferred until later. Communication will be key here, especially with all the moving parts we're managing."

Sarah nodded, her tone softening slightly. *"Adewale makes a good point. We'll need to collaborate closely to avoid any gaps. If we're not careful, this transition could create more problems than it solves."*

Gaby leaned back in his chair, his expression thoughtful. *"I hear you all, and I appreciate the candid feedback. Let's agree to meet again tomorrow to review Adewale's transition plan in detail. We'll also schedule a separate session with the new team to evaluate their preparedness. Does that sound reasonable?"*

I unmuted once again, glancing around at the team. "The reason I emphasized communication earlier is because I believe it's crucial to keep our stakeholders in the loop during this transition. Transparency will ensure we're aligned and prevent any surprises down the line. As we schedule the follow-up meeting and the session with the new team, I recommend we also schedule a meeting with the stakeholders to inform them about the changes. We need to ensure they're not left in the dark."

Sarah was the first to respond, her brow furrowed. *"I see your point, Adewale, but I'm not sure informing the stakeholders right now is the best move. Given the tight timeline and the uncertainty surrounding the transition, I'm concerned they might panic. We might be better off waiting until we have a clearer picture before sharing anything with them."*

Khalid joined in, his voice cautious. *"I agree with Sarah. While keeping them informed seems like the right approach in theory, I think it's risky at this stage. The stakeholders could become anxious if they feel like the change is happening too quickly or without enough information. It might be better to hold off and only inform them once we have more concrete details."*

Gaby nodded, his expression thoughtful but hesitant. *"I understand the rationale behind keeping them in the loop, but I'm leaning toward waiting. If we tell them too soon, they might start questioning the decision, and that could create unnecessary concern. We don't want to make the situation more volatile than it already is."*

I leaned back in my chair, trying to gather my thoughts. I knew I had to find a way to convince them about the importance of transparency, especially when it came to our stakeholders. After a brief pause, I spoke again, my tone more measured. "Gaby, remember the primary reason we're even considering this transition is to ensure the long-term sustainability of the project. The goal is to have an internal team with the right experience and stability. But at the same time, we're an Agile team, and as such, we must be honest and transparent. We're doing Scrum, and we've committed to sprinting, delivering shippable product increments at the end of each sprint… no matter how small. Our stakeholders are expecting that. If we don't communicate these changes to them, they will notice. The disruption will be more obvious than we think."

I paused for a moment to let that sink in. "In fact, if the team doesn't deliver anything by the end of this sprint, our stakeholders are going to be furious. They won't understand why there was no increment, and that's when the lack of transparency will bite us. Everyone will know this sprint will mostly be for knowledge transfer between the incoming team and the contractors. We all know this transition will impact development, and the progress won't be as visible. But if we don't inform the stakeholders upfront, they'll be blindsided."

I looked at each of them to emphasize my point. "At least if the stakeholders know what's going on, they won't be surprised at the end of the sprint when no deliverable is ready. They'll have been prepared for the slowdown, and they'll understand the reasons behind it. That way, the transparency actually builds trust, rather than eroding it."

I could see that the wheels were turning in their minds. They understood the weight of what I was saying, but the reservation was still there. They were concerned about how to communicate this to the stakeholders, but at least my perspective had helped shift their mindset.

I leaned back in my chair, taking a moment to gather my thoughts. I knew I had their attention now, and this was my chance to change their mindset. I paused for a moment, making eye contact with each of them before continuing. "I also want to remind you of Agile Principle #4: 'Business people and developers must work together daily throughout the project.' This isn't just a guideline – It's a core principle. Any change or decision that affects the project should be communicated to all those involved, including the stakeholders. If we withhold this information from them, we're essentially violating that principle."

Sarah conceded. *"Thank you, Adewale,"* she sounded convinced. *"But we don't want to cause unnecessary concern. Maybe we should wait until we have a solid plan in place, then inform them,"* she suggested.

Khalid nodded in agreement. *"I think it's wise to have a strategy for how we'll manage the transition smoothly before informing them,"* he said. *"We need to ensure we can still meet our commitments,"* he added.

Gaby responded, *"Thank you, Adewale. That was a great call-out. And thanks, Sarah and Khalid, for your input. I think we can find a balance here. We'll inform them about the transition, but we'll also reassure them that we have a solid plan in place to ensure a smooth process."*

The Microsoft Teams notification popped up, reminding us that there were just five minutes left in the meeting. I paused for a second, feeling the weight of the decision settling in. "I agree that having a plan is essential," I began, "but I also believe we can start by informing them about the transition and reassuring them that we are prepared. Our transparency will build trust, and our plan will demonstrate our commitment to success. Highlighting the long-term benefits and our commitment to quality should help alleviate their concerns. Let's work together to create a clear plan and present it to the stakeholders."

"The reason I want us to inform the stakeholders now is that we want them to feel involved in the decision-making process. By keeping them in the loop while we work on the plan, we show that we value their input and ensure they're part of the solution."

As the meeting came to a close, it was clear that everyone was aligned on the importance of keeping the stakeholders in the loop. Gaby planned to schedule a follow-up meeting for the next day to discuss the transition plan in more detail. I agreed to schedule a call with the important stakeholders and another meeting with the incoming team.

I asked Gaby to share with me the names and IDs of the new team members so I could set up a meeting with them. We both agreed that Gaby's meeting would take precedence, as it was critical for us to align on the transition plan, which would lay the foundation for the next two meetings – one with the new team and the other with the stakeholders.

The next day, Gaby, Sarah, Khalid, and I met in our virtual conference room as planned. The early morning sunlight streamed through my home office window, casting a warm glow over the room, creating a sense of calm before what I knew would be a challenging discussion. I noticed the determined expressions on everyone's faces as they joined the call.

Gaby's approach had always been optimistic. *"It's all about framing it as an investment,"* she had said earlier, and she truly believed that. Sarah, on the other hand, had been more cautious. She didn't like the idea of being transparent with stakeholders about the delays. *"What if they don't understand? What if they lose faith in us?"* she asked, a question that reflected her fear of losing trust. Khalid was more neutral. He understood both sides but knew the risks of pushing forward without proper preparation. *"We have to explain the bigger picture,"* he reminded us.

"Alright, team," I began, glancing at my notes, "we need to align on how to approach the knowledge transfer and manage the potential impact on the sprint goal." We all understood that this transition would be pivotal in the success of the team and the project, and keeping our stakeholders informed was paramount to navigating the next steps smoothly.

Gaby leaned forward, her background showing a whiteboard filled with scribbles. *"I think we need to be upfront about this. It's clear the team will spend this sprint on knowledge transfer, which means we won't be delivering any significant increment."*

Khalid nodded but hesitated before speaking. *"Agreed, but we should be ready for pushback. Stakeholders might not like hearing about delays, especially if it affects the timeline or scope."*

"You're right," Sarah added, a hint of concern in her voice. *"We'll need a solid explanation for why this is necessary and what the long-term benefits are."*

"Exactly," I interjected. "Our priority should be transparency and collaboration. By clearly explaining the situation and highlighting the benefits of this transition, I'm confident they'll understand. We should also be ready to address any concerns about timelines and scope."

As I watched Sarah and Khalid, I could sense the pressure they were under. The idea of having to communicate potential setbacks to stakeholders wasn't easy for either of them. But their professionalism shone through. Khalid, always the practical one, kept his concerns to himself during the meeting, while Sarah was visibly stressed, despite agreeing with our strategy. She glanced at me during our discussion, as if seeking reassurance. It wasn't just about the delay; it was about keeping trust with stakeholders while guiding the new team through a critical transition.

"Let's also address the elephant in the room," I said, breaking the silence as I typed up our notes. "Any concerns about the stakeholders?"

Khalid raised his concern. *"What if they push back and insist on sticking to the original sprint goals?"*

I paused, frowning slightly. "Then we'll need to stand firm and explain why pushing forward without this knowledge transfer could cause more harm than good."

By the end of the meeting, we were aligned. We agreed to communicate to stakeholders that the sprint would primarily focus on knowledge transfer and that incremental delivery might not happen this time. To reassure them, we prepared responses to potential questions about the timeline and scope, focusing on how this step would ultimately lead to greater success.

The next meeting with the stakeholders came up, and we gathered with some of our key stakeholders to explain the current situation. We began by emphasizing the long-term benefits of ensuring stability in the team and the experience of the new members. Gaby led the discussion, clearly outlining how this knowledge transfer would set the team up for success. The stakeholders were very appreciative that we kept them in the loop and valued our collaboration. They could see the rationale behind our approach, which was a relief.

Their only concern was the timeline, as they had hoped for a more tangible deliverable. We addressed this concern by explaining that the knowledge transfer was necessary to avoid future bottlenecks. They appreciated the transparency and the clear communication about the potential risks of pushing forward too quickly. The stakeholders were okay with not receiving any increment this sprint and advised us to reach out to them for any support during the process. They were pleased to be part of the decision-making process and reassured us that they trusted our approach.

With the stakeholder meeting behind us, we quickly transitioned to the incoming team, where we shared the background and set expectations for the knowledge transfer. It was essential to ease them into the process smoothly, so everyone understood what needed to happen next. I recognized one of the new team members from a previous project we had worked on together. She's an excellent tester with a lot of knowledge. We were both happy to see each other again.

After everyone was aligned, I shared the meeting invites for the daily stand-ups, backlog refinements, and other Scrum ceremonies to ensure they would be up to speed.

Throughout the sprint, both the incoming and outgoing teams worked closely together to ensure a smooth knowledge transfer. The collaboration between them was essential to laying a strong foundation for the new team's success. The daily touchpoints between the two teams kept everyone aligned and helped reinforce our commitment to collaboration and transparency.

At the end of the sprint, we held a retrospective meeting, the room filled with a sense of gratitude. The outgoing team's contributions were acknowledged, and the incoming team's excitement to step up was palpable. It felt like the end of one chapter and the beginning of another. The gratitude shared among everyone made me reflect on how important it was to keep things transparent every step of the way.

The new team also took the opportunity to thank the outgoing team for their support and collaboration during the knowledge transfer process. This mutual respect further reinforced the strength of our teamwork and the positive impact of clear communication.

As expected, we were unable to deliver any increment by the end of the sprint, and we informed the stakeholders of this without issue. Fortunately, the stakeholders were understanding, knowing that the new team needed time to get up to speed with the application. The new team started the following sprint with high hopes of delivering value, but the reality was that they were still familiarizing themselves with the system.

I reminded Sarah and Khalid about the importance of ongoing communication with stakeholders. Reflecting on the past few weeks, I could see how keeping them in the loop had helped us manage expectations and avoid unnecessary pressure. Without their awareness and understanding of the situation, we could have easily found ourselves under pressure. They both agreed, acknowledging that the only reason we weren't facing undue pressure was because the stakeholders were fully aware of the changes and the potential impact. They had no unrealistic expectations about the new team delivering value immediately.

By the third sprint, the new team started hitting their stride. Their confidence grew as they began to understand the system better. We finally delivered our first increment since the transition, and it was exactly what the stakeholders had hoped for. It wasn't just the technical success that mattered, but the success in terms of collaboration and alignment. The stakeholders saw the potential of the team, and their trust in our approach grew.

Reflecting back on the entire process, it was clear that Principle #4 was at the heart of our success. We didn't just 'get by' through the transition; we succeeded because of the constant collaboration, the transparent communication, and the shared goal of delivering value. The stakeholders remained patient because they trusted us, and that trust was built through our honesty and commitment to the team. In the end, this was the key to our success… ensuring everyone worked together toward a common goal, despite the challenges.

Takeaway for Readers:
Business people and developers must work together daily throughout the project.

Keeping stakeholders informed is crucial, not just during transitions or major changes, but throughout the entire project lifecycle, whether progress is smooth or obstacles arise. Transparency and collaboration proved to be our greatest allies. By consistently updating stakeholders on any changes, we aligned expectations and built a solid foundation of trust.

Even when facing challenges and missing sprint targets, our stakeholders remained supportive. They appreciated our honesty and the commitment to keeping them in the loop. If we had withheld information, missed deadlines might have led to frustration and mistrust. Instead, we turned a potentially difficult situation into an opportunity to strengthen our partnership and reinforce the importance of collaboration.

Chapter 5
The Power of Stepping Back

It was a Tuesday morning, the sun just beginning to peek through the blinds, casting a warm glow across the room. Outside, the summer heat lingered, but inside, the comfort of fresh coffee and the low hum of conversations mixed with the steady whir of the projector.

I was working with a Scrum team focused on building and refining software for a critical release. Our work was organized in short, time-boxed sprints, each one carrying us closer to the holiday deadline.

The project carried a critical timeline. With Thanksgiving fast approaching and only a few iterations left in our cadence, the pressure was mounting.

North American stakeholders had one clear goal: ensure the application was ready for the holiday season, the company's peak customer engagement period. The stakes were high, and everyone in the room felt it. This wasn't just another backlog refinement, every decision carried weight.

Among those present was Jacob, a senior IT manager and one of our most influential stakeholders. Known for his sharp, no-nonsense style, he often brought intensity to these sessions, most times helpful, sometimes disruptive.

Jacob was always present at these meetings, sitting at the table serving as the Chair, meticulously scrutinizing every detail and asking a barrage of questions. While his intentions were always to keep things on track, his constant interference was starting to create friction. I remembered a past session where his constant questioning of the team's estimates had caused delays. The team had spent over an hour re-explaining their thought process, which ultimately led to a loss of focus and momentum. It was becoming clear that the team was struggling to keep up with his pace, and their confidence was beginning to falter.

While his interruptions sometimes disrupted the flow, his ability to identify overlooked risks or suggest alternative approaches often proved valuable. I remembered a previous session where he pointed out a potential dependency that the team hadn't considered, ultimately saving us time and effort later. Yet, the challenge was finding a way to channel his insights without letting them overshadow the team's autonomy.

Tracy, our Product Owner (PO), was also in the room. Having worked with Jacob on previous projects, she knew him well. As always, she sat quietly beside him, maintaining an attentive posture, her occasional glance reflecting her familiarity with his style and her anticipation of what was to come.

There was shared determination and anticipation in the room, a recognition that their efforts were pivotal to meeting the stakeholders' expectations.

The backlog refinement meeting was in full swing, with team members gathered in the conference room and others joining virtually from offshore. Tracy, our PO, greeted everyone with a warm smile, her eyes scanning the room. *"How are we progressing with the technical uncertainties on some of these user stories?"* she asked, her voice light but purposeful. *"Is there a resolution to what we're refining today? I need to understand if this will fit into our next deliverables."* She spoke with a sense of hope, always focused on ensuring the team could meet their targets.

Arun, the backend engineer, explained the technical complexity of a user story, which the team had estimated at 13 story points. As the conversation unfolded, Tracy's quiet presence continued to anchor the room. She leaned slightly forward, her pen moving steadily across her notebook as she jotted down key points from the discussion.

Occasionally, she would nod subtly, her expression affirming the team's insights without interrupting their flow. It was her way of signaling trust with a silent acknowledgment that she valued their expertise and was aligned with their approach.

Before anyone could respond, Jacob interrupted, as I expected. *"Why is this estimated at 13 story points? This doesn't seem like it should take that long. Why can't we implement a quicker solution with the existing architecture?"*

His sharp pushback reminded me of my very first encounter with him during my interview, the same direct, no-fluff questions that cut straight to the point. That day, I learned Jacob always came ready to challenge assumptions.

The room went quiet. Arun looked at Jacob, a mix of confusion and frustration on his face. But Jacob wasn't finished. His gaze swept across the table, and he pushed further, *"Are you sure about this? This really doesn't seem like a 13-point story. You're telling me it's going to take more than a week of work to implement? I think we're overestimating here."*

The team shifted uneasily, the pressure mounting. Arun tried to explain once more, his voice steady but tense. *"The current system can't support this integration. The new architecture is necessary for security and scalability. It's not a matter of overestimating, it's about doing it right."*

Jacob frowned, clearly dissatisfied. *"So, we need to build a new architecture just for this? That seems excessive."*

Arun nodded. *"Yes, it's necessary for long-term success. Rushing this could compromise everything."*

Jacob, still unconvinced, glanced around the room. "*Does anyone else agree with Arun, or are we overestimating things?"* he asked, his tone sharp.

Jindu, the Quality Assurance (QA) engineer, spoke up cautiously. *"I think Arun's right. If we rush this, we could face bigger issues down the line."*

Jacob's expression hardened, but before he could press further, Tracy's voice broke through. *"We've worked through the complexity here, Jacob. I believe Arun and the team are right on track,"* she said softly, but firmly.

To be fair, his intensity wasn't always destructive. In an earlier session, he had spotted a hidden dependency the team overlooked, saving us weeks of rework. The challenge was never his intelligence, it was knowing how to channel it without overshadowing the team.

Arun, sensing her support, gave a small nod in her direction, a quiet gesture that spoke volumes about the team's trust in Tracy's judgment.

The tension in the room grew. This wasn't the first time Jacob had pushed for quick solutions, questioning the team's expertise and rushing estimates. His interference was starting to take a toll, especially since some of the team members were contractors who didn't always feel comfortable pushing back.

I could see the discomfort in the team's eyes. The pressure was building, and I knew I needed to step in.

In that silence, I realized this wasn't just about estimation, it was about trust. Jacob's constant challenges weren't only slowing us down, they were shaking the team's confidence. What we needed in that moment was space for the team to own their decisions.

As I considered how to handle Jacob's behavior, one Agile principle came to mind: Principle #5: "Build projects around motivated individuals. Give them the environment and support they need, and trust them to get the job done."

I messaged Jacob on Microsoft Teams: "Jacob, I understand your concerns, but let the team handle the estimation without pressure. We'll discuss the architecture afterward."

Jacob read the message and nodded silently. I knew he was still skeptical, but at least the tension was defused, for now. Turning to the team, I reassured them, "We've got this. Just focus on the work and trust the process."

The team visibly relaxed, their confidence restored. The meeting continued without further disruption, and the team's sense of control was reestablished.

After the meeting, I sent Jacob a quick message on Microsoft Teams: "Hi Jacob, do you have a minute to chat?"

"Sure," he replied.

I waited for the other team members to leave, the sound of their chatter fading into the distance. Then, I approached him carefully, my heart beating slightly faster.

"Jacob," I said, my voice low and even, "I can see how invested you are in the team's success. That's commendable." I paused, studying his expression. "But I think we're missing out on something important. We need to trust the team to take ownership."

He raised an eyebrow, skeptical. I continued, "What if we tried an experiment? For the next two sprints, let's give the team the environment and support they need – the time, space, and freedom to refine without interference – and let them run the sessions on their own. I'll be there to guide them, and you can step back to observe the results. "Let's see what they can do when we give them the space to thrive."

Jacob hesitated. *"You really think this will work?"*

"I do," I replied confidently. "Trust me on this one."

Reluctantly, Jacob agreed. For the next two sprints, the team would operate independently.

Without Jacob's constant interference, the team began to engage in the refinement sessions with newfound confidence. Instead of hesitating under scrutiny, they spoke with clarity and ownership.

Arun took the lead in explaining each user story's technical complexity. *"This integration isn't just plug-and-play,"* he said. *"We'll need extra configuration for security and scalability."*

Paul jumped in from the front-end perspective. "If we change that Application Programming Interface (API) call, I'll need a few extra days to adjust the UI components – but it's doable if we align dependencies early."

Jindu leaned forward, adding his concerns. *"From QA's side, we'll need time to test the edge cases. If we skip that, we'll run into trouble later."*

Even the offshore team chimed in over video. *"We can cover the overnight regression tests,"* one member suggested, *"so you'll have results ready by morning."*

The conversation flowed smoothly, each voice building on the other. For the first time in weeks, there were no interruptions, no second-guessing, just open, confident collaboration.

At our follow-up refinement session, the difference was clear. The team carried the conversation with ease, no hesitation, no glances toward Jacob for approval.

Arun started confidently: *"This API will take some extra effort, the authentication layer is different from what we've used before."*

Paul nodded thoughtfully. *"That means I'll need to adjust the UI workflow. If Arun needs a few extra points, I think it's justified, we'd rather size this right than cut corners."*

Jindu added his perspective. *"As long as we account for those changes, I can design test cases around it. I'd recommend we size this at 8 story points."*

Arun agreed. *"Eight sounds right to me."*

The team exchanged quick nods. Consensus came quickly, without long debates or outside pressure, a striking contrast to how things had been before.

The offshore team members, connected via video, actively contributed as well, ensuring that time zone differences didn't slow them down. Everyone worked collaboratively to assess the complexity and called out dependencies of each user story.

The flow of the conversation was smooth and efficient. There was no tension, no one second-guessing the estimates, no interruption from outside pressure. Arun, Paul, Jindu, and the others reached a consensus on each story's size, and the estimation process felt almost effortless. The energy in the room shifted from anxious to productive.

As the sprints unfolded, Jacob's absence became a catalyst for transformation. The team grew more empowered, taking ownership of the refinement sessions with a newfound energy. Even Jacob began to notice the efficiency and collaboration emerging within the team. *"It's interesting,"* he remarked during a casual chat. *"They're more proactive now, tackling issues without hesitation. Maybe stepping back was the right call after all."*

During each session, the team moved smoothly through the backlog, discussing each story, debating where it should fit in the sprint, and coming to a consensus on its relative size. Instead of tense back-and-forth, their conversations carried an easy rhythm.

The team's collaboration was also a living example of another Agile insight – Principle #11: "The best architectures, requirements, and designs emerge from self-organizing teams." With Jacob stepping back, the team naturally organized around the work, debated solutions openly, and discovered better approaches together. We'll dive deeper into Principle #11 in Chapter 11, where you'll see how it reinforces and builds upon Principle #5, the core focus of this chapter.

Their energy was unmistakable – meetings that once dragged now flowed, and their delivery soared. Conversations had rhythm, decisions came faster, and the team worked with a confidence that hadn't been there before. This transformation was largely driven by the team refining every detail of user stories autonomously before pulling them into the sprint, without interference from outsiders. That autonomy ensured each story was clear and well understood, enabling the team to work with greater focus and effectiveness during execution. By the end of the experiment, the numbers confirmed it: nearly 55% more than in previous sprints.

Seeing the team thrive reminded me of coaching a soccer team. As a coach, you can shout instructions from the sidelines all game long, but real growth happens when you trust the players to make decisions on the field. Sometimes they stumble, sometimes they surprise you. But either way, they learn, adapt, and own the outcome. Work teams aren't so different. Trust creates the space for them to rise, and when they do, the results often exceed expectations.

Jacob couldn't believe the results. "*I didn't think stepping back would make such a difference,*" he admitted during our follow-up conversation. As the weeks went on, Jacob began to change his approach in meetings, asking the team more open-ended questions and encouraging them to take ownership of decisions. He even became a vocal advocate for giving teams more autonomy in future projects, sharing his experience with others and championing the idea that trust and empowerment lead to better results.

The team not only met the critical deadline but also completed the project a sprint ahead of schedule. Users were able to engage with the application just in time for the Thanksgiving holiday, achieving the stakeholders' goals seamlessly. Jacob, once a skeptical and intense stakeholder, transformed into a smiling advocate, expressing his gratitude and admiration for the team's exceptional performance.

Takeaway for Readers:
Build projects around motivated individuals. Give them the environment and support they need, and trust them to get the job done.

Trust is the foundation of empowerment. Once you've created the right environment and support, stepping back gives your team the space to take ownership and unlock their true potential.

Jacob's story shows that micromanaging slows progress, while trust fuels autonomy, accountability and collaboration — the essence of Agile Principle #5. This same trust also lays the groundwork for self-organization, a theme we'll revisit in Chapter 11. For now, remember when you strike the right balance between guidance and space, your team will deliver remarkable result.

Chapter 6
The Power of Face-to-Face Conversation and How Connection Beats Assumption

It was a Saturday evening, and my cousin, Arewa, and I had planned to meet and reconnect over the weekend. We hadn't seen each other in months, and this was our chance to unwind, catch up on life, and talk about everything from work to family. But as we approached the bar, I couldn't shake the feeling that something was off. Arewa's usual lively energy seemed dimmed, his shoulders just a little stiffer than usual. We met in front of the Golden 1 Center in downtown Sacramento, just a three-minute walk from one of the most popular sports bars in the area.

As we walked in, the dim glow of the bar lights flickered over the polished wooden counter as Arewa, and I settled into our seats. The air buzzed with conversations, the occasional clink of glasses, and the distant hum of music weaving through the background. It was supposed to be a chill night, just two cousins catching up, but the tension in Arewa's face told a different story.

A Sacramento Kings vs. Miami Heat game played on the TV, with the bartender, clearly a die-hard fan, shaking his head at every missed shot.

"You guys watching this? Kings got a real shot this season," the bartender said.

Arewa and I exchanged a glance. We weren't basketball fans. We were soccer guys through and through.

But we also didn't want to be disrespectful. So instead of engaging, we stylistically redirected the conversation.

Arewa ordered his usual Long Island Iced Tea, tapping his fingers impatiently as the bartender poured. I asked for an Old-Fashioned, a slow sipper for the kind of night I thought we were about to have.

No more basketball talk. The slow rhythm of calypso and reggae music played softly in the background. The smooth basslines and island beats gave the bar a laid-back vibe, a contrast to the intense energy on the TV screen.

But even as the music played and the drinks settled in front of us, I could tell, Arewa wasn't really in the moment. His mind was elsewhere.

He had been arguing with his girlfriend earlier that day. Nothing serious, just one of those back-and-forth exchanges that every couple goes through. But in an attempt to smooth things over, he invited her to join us at the bar. She agreed, saying she'd be there in twenty minutes. Wanting to lighten the mood before she arrived, he started sending her funny Instagram memes – Inside jokes they'd often shared.

A few minutes later, she responded with a short text:

"You are so stupid."

Arewa's mood snapped like a rubber band. His jaw clenched, fingers tightening around his phone. He read the message again. And again. His eyes darted across the screen, as if some hidden meaning would suddenly reveal itself.

"Why would she say that?" he muttered with wounded pride. *"I'm just trying to make things right, and she's being disrespectful?"*

I watched him, already recognizing the pattern – the impact of the message was completely overriding the sender's original intent. For Arewa, being Nigerian, words perceived as challenging intelligence or respect were not casually exchanged as affectionate jokes.

I took a sip of my drink and shrugged. "Maybe she's just joking?"

He shook his head sharply. *"No, this is different. Why would she say that after everything?"*

We waited. Twenty minutes passed. Then forty. Then a full hour. No sign of her. No follow-up messages. Arewa's frustration grew. His fingers drummed against the bar, the ice in his drink melting untouched. He was convinced now, she wasn't coming. That message, he believed, was her way of brushing him off.

At that point, I suggested, "Let's not assume. Let's step outside and give her a call."

Reluctantly, he agreed. We walked out of the bar, and he dialed her number on FaceTime. The phone rang twice before she picked up.

Her face appeared on the screen, smiling. *"Hey baby! I'm on my way! My tire got messed up on the freeway, and I had to call a tow truck. They just fixed it. I should be there in seven minutes!"*

In an instant, all the stories he had spun in his head unraveled. She hadn't been ignoring him. She wasn't upset. The text – the one he'd obsessed over for an hour – had meant nothing at all. A joke. Had he just picked up the phone sooner, he could have saved himself the stress, the frustration, and the melted ice in his untouched drink.

Arewa let out a deep sigh and chuckled, *"Man… I almost ruined my own night over nothing."*

That moment reminded me of one of the core principles of Agile: "The most efficient and effective method of conveying information to and within a development team is face-to-face conversation."

But this principle isn't confined to software teams, it's universal. Whether in personal life, family settings, or any profession, clear conversation prevents misunderstandings and strengthens trust.

As I sat there, watching Arewa spiral into frustration over a simple text message, I couldn't help but think about how often this happens in the workplace. Just like he misinterpreted a casual message from his girlfriend, teams sometimes misinterpret written communication.

Misunderstandings thrive in silence but vanish in conversation. Just like Arewa cleared up everything the second he saw his girlfriend's face on the call. Agile teams avoid wasted energy when they prioritize direct conversations.

This can easily occur when teams rely too much on written communication. Without vocal tone, facial expressions, or body language, messages can be misread or taken out of context. A simple phrase intended as a joke may come across as rude, and a straightforward request might feel like a demand.

How often have you sent an email that was misread, or received a Slack message that felt colder than intended? Without tone, emotion, or context, written words are easily misinterpreted, creating unnecessary friction in teams.

This is why Agile emphasizes real-time conversations. A simple voice or video chat can resolve in minutes what endless emails cannot – bringing trust, clarity and alignment back to the team. Instead of making assumptions, direct conversations foster trust and alignment.

In today's fast-paced and often remote work environments, ensuring seamless communication is more important than ever. While Agile originally emphasized in-person discussions, modern teams must adapt by leveraging video calls, real-time messaging, and intentional check-ins to maintain clarity and human connection.

And this principle doesn't stand alone. It directly complements one of the four core Agile values:

"Individuals and interactions over processes and tools."

Emails, Slack, and project management tools have their place – but they should support, not replace human interaction. You could send ten emails back and forth, trying to clarify a point, or you could resolve it in seconds with a quick conversation. The difference is understanding vs. assumption.

Just like Arewa and his girlfriend cleared things up the moment they saw each other's expressions, teams work more effectively when they prioritize direct communication. In professional settings, visual cues such as facial expressions, gestures, and tone of voice help clarify intent, reduce misunderstandings, and build trust. When teams engage in video calls or face-to-face conversations, they gain insights that text-based communication simply cannot provide. A five-minute conversation can often resolve what might take twenty emails. Whether it's a one-on-one video call, a quick stand-up meeting, or an in-person discussion, talking things through ensures alignment and minimizes confusion.

Agile isn't just about following processes – It's about collaboration and clarity. Teams thrive when they see and hear each other, whether in-person or virtually. Emails should inform, but conversations should align. When misunderstandings happen, don't assume – talk it out. That's how Agile teams build trust, move faster, and deliver better results.

Watching Arewa clear things up with one call made me think of another time when silence bred assumptions – inside my own team, with one of our brightest team members, David.

David thrived in our culture of face-to-face interaction. I always encouraged the team to turn their cameras on during meetings – not as a rule, but as a way to build stronger connections. When people showed up visually, the energy shifted. Trust grew, collaboration flowed, and the team felt more connected. David embodied that spirit effortlessly. Brilliant, energetic, and quick to laugh, he lit up our Scrum ceremonies. He cracked jokes, checked in on team members, and his presence gave our meetings a heartbeat.

But his impact went deeper than personality. During backlog refinement and sprint planning, he was fully engaged, often bridging gaps between the Business Analyst and Product Owner (PO). He clarified requirements, offered solutions, and his enthusiasm showed in every smile and gesture on camera. David didn't just contribute technically, he made the team feel alive.

Then something changed. Subtle at first, just a missing video feed. At first, no one thought much of it. But then came other shifts. David, once quick to respond on Teams, now lagged. Messages that used to get replies in minutes dragged into hours. The late-night email acceptance at 11:30 PM was my red flag. Was he overworked? Disengaged? Or was it something else?

Meetings grew quieter. The easy banter faded. And though no one said it out loud, the void was felt. That's when I stepped in, not with assumptions, but with a conversation.

I called David for a one-on-one. We started lighthearted, trading football banter (him being a Manchester United fan, me a Liverpool fan, always good for a laugh). Then I leaned in:

"Hey, I noticed you've been off camera lately. If your laptop's broken, do you want me to pay for a new one?" I joked.

He chuckled, but then sighed. "Honestly… I just moved. My home office isn't set up yet, and the internet's been unreliable. I figured keeping the camera off was easier for now."

At that moment, all the assumptions others had been making, "he's checked out", "he's unhappy", "maybe he's job hunting" fell apart. It wasn't disengagement at all. It was logistics. Moving stress. Internet issues. Life.

The next day, he shared his situation with the team. They understood, checked in on him, and the awkward silence that had crept into meetings began to fade. Slowly, he re-engaged. His camera stayed off for a while, but his voice grew stronger. And then, one meeting later, his camera flickered back on. The reactions were immediate:

"David! Good to see you, man!"

"Glad you're back."

It wasn't just his face on screen. It was the energy coming back into the team.

That experience reinforced a truth I'll never forget communication isn't just about words, it's about presence. When someone withdraws, even quietly, the whole team feels it. In Agile settings, where collaboration is everything, silence is a risk. That's why leaders, Scrum Masters, Agile Project Managers, Agile Coaches, and others in similar roles must read the room. When someone goes quiet, whether by turning off a camera, slowing responses or fading from discussions, it's a signal. Not to assume, but to ask.

Presence isn't optional – it's essential. And it's not just about who is speaking, but also about who is silently withdrawing.

I've seen developers, product owners, and even senior leaders slowly withdraw from team interactions, not because they're unhappy, but because something external is going on. They might be dealing with personal struggles, feeling burnt out, or simply adjusting to a new work environment.

But here's the problem, when someone pulls back, the whole team feels it. Conversations lose their spark. Decisions stall. Collaboration weakens, not because people don't care, but because they hesitate, unsure of the silence. Before you know it, misunderstandings replace clarity, and assumptions become the team's new reality.

In a collaborative Agile ecosystem, transparency is everything. When the continuous flow of communication and contribution slows, we instantly lose visibility – and that is a major risk to predictability and morale. A leader must maintain constant situational awareness and inspect the team's behavioral cues. Whether the camera is switched off, the chat activity that begins to dwindle, or the detailed responses that become lean. These are not inconveniences; they are calls to action. They signal a need to proactively close that visibility gap and facilitate a supportive, targeted check-in, because the ultimate is to protect the health of your system.

And more often than not, a simple, *"Hey, I noticed you've been a little quiet. Is everything okay?"* can make all the difference.

Agile Principle No. 6 teaches us that the best way to communicate is through direct conversation, but beyond that, it reminds us that teams thrive when they feel connected. It isn't just about efficiency- it's about emotional intelligence.

Tools like email and Slack are useful, but trust and clarity come from real conversations – whether across a desk or through a quick voice or video call.

Now, let's leave Agile aside for a second.

Think about any job, any career. Ever had an interview over email? Of course not.

Nope. Never. It's always a video call or an in-person conversation. Why? Because companies know that seeing and talking to someone directly tells you way more than words on a screen ever could.

So, if face-to-face interaction is important enough to determine who gets hired, why wouldn't it be just as important when we're already working together – especially in a remote setting, where connection can easily fade?

At the core of Agile is people over processes. And people work best when they see, hear, and understand each other, not just through messages, but through real human connection. If you want a team that thrives, don't just rely on emails – talk to your people.

If you're leading a team, pay attention to presence. Cameras aren't about rules, they're about connection. Because in Agile, connection isn't optional, it's essential.

Create space for informal talks. Sometimes, a casual conversation before a meeting can uncover what a dozen emails never will. A few minutes of real conversation can prevent days of misalignment.

The tools we use are important, but the connections we build with each other are what truly make teams successful.

Agile thrives on conversation, not speculation. That's how trust is built.

Takeaway for Readers:
The most efficient and effective method of conveying information to and within a development team is face-to-face conversation.

Arewa's misinterpretation and David's silence highlight a simple truth: Assumptions thrive when connection fades, but clarity comes from conversation. In Agile and beyond, communication is more than just words. It is about presence, connection, and genuine human interaction. Whether it's clearing up a misread message like Arewa's or addressing a team member's withdrawal like David's, the solution remains the same.

Don't assume… Ask. Don't speculate… Connect. This chapter reinforces the importance of face-to-face communication in eliminating assumptions and bringing true understanding.

Agile was built on face-to-face collaboration. Today, video calls, real-time check-ins, and intentional conversations ensure that human connection isn't lost. It just looks different.

Chapter 7
The Power of What Works: Piece by Piece, Progress by Progress

As we reflect on the journey that brought me to Agile principles, one stands out – not just as a professional milestone, but as a personal revelation rooted in the lessons I learned from my father. This chapter is a deeply personal exploration of how the concept of measuring progress through working components first took root in my mind, long before I ever heard the term "Agile."

During this chapter, and especially by the end of this story, you might understand how a formative experience from my father's workshop introduced me to one of the core Agile principles and laid the foundation for how I define effective progress. This early lesson – ensuring every component functions independently before integration – was my first real exposure to a concept I would later recognize as a cornerstone of the Software Development Life Cycle (SDLC). As you delve deeper, you'll see how this principle not only shaped my professional mindset but also became a guiding force in my approach to both life and work.

Growing up, I had the privilege of working alongside my father, a skilled welder who specialized in building agricultural machines such as cassava graters, pepper grinders, and maize grinders, among others. Each machine was made up of many components, and my father's unwavering principle was clear: every part had to function flawlessly on its own before it became part of the whole.

Our workshop was always alive with movement and noise. Sparks flew from multiple corners at once, hammers rang out rhythmically, and the clatter of metal on metal echoed all day long. The sharp smell of hot metal and oil hung in the air, mixing with the heat from welding flames. Everyone had their hands full – each of us focused on a different component of a machine in progress. Sometimes, there was pressure to deliver and meet the timelines of his customers. Despite the constant activity and urgency, my father never allowed quality to be compromised.

For him, this wasn't just a job – it was a system, a craft, a standard he refused to compromise. Even in the middle of that busyness, he insisted that every piece we worked on met his expectations. He often walked from station to station, inspecting parts himself, reminding us: "It must work on its own before it becomes part of the whole." No exceptions. If a pulley didn't rotate smoothly, it got scrapped. If a blade didn't cut right, it was redone. To him, a job was only as good as its weakest part.

That discipline taught us an important truth: real progress wasn't measured by speed or by the number of machines delivered – it was measured by how well each part performed, both independently and together. At the time, my father had nearly twenty apprentices in his workshop. Some had already completed their training but stayed on to deepen their skills. Others were on short-term contracts, while a few, like me and my younger brother, were still learning the craft from the ground up.

Sometimes, a single person would work on a component from start to finish. Other times, it could take two, three, four, or even five people to complete one part, depending on the effort and complexity involved. Everyone played a role, and collaboration was constant.

Looking back, I now see how this dynamic mirrors the rhythm of a software development team. Just like in our workshop, developers may shift between groups or pair up to solve problems. Sometimes we learn by working independently; other times we grow through collaboration – much like pair programming.

At the time, I just thought that was the way things had to be. But years later, in my career as an Agile Project Manager, I realized my father had been teaching us one of the most important principles in software and systems development: working software, or a working product, is the true measure of progress.

He ingrained this philosophy in everyone who worked with him, including his apprentices. Each component underwent rigorous checks and tests to ensure it met quality standards before it was integrated into the final product. This meticulous focus on quality set him apart from competitors who often rushed to assemble and deliver their machines without thorough testing.

Despite having only a basic education, my father consistently outperformed competitors with higher degrees. While many of them invested time in writing detailed manuals and making their machines look polished and luxurious, he focused on what truly mattered: a product that worked, built for long-term reliability and sustainability.

Don't get me wrong, some competitors delivered quality. But I often saw customers bring in faulty machines bought elsewhere, asking my father to rebuild them. What struck me most was that the original makers, despite their formal education, had overlooked the simplest, most essential thing: building a machine that actually worked.

The first thing my father would tell us to do was disassemble the machine entirely, take it apart piece by piece. Then, we'd test each component independently to ensure it worked as it should before reassembling everything into a final product. Looking back, I now compare this to unit testing and regression testing in today's world of software development. His approach naturally complements one of the Agile principles that values working software over comprehensive documentation.

This method not only ensured that his customers received reliable, high-quality products, but it also earned him a reputation for excellence and helped his business thrive. Watching my father uphold this standard resonated with me deeply. It taught me that the primary measure of progress is not just completing a task or delivering a product, but ensuring that each part of the process works effectively and independently.

This lesson mirrors Agile Principle #7: working software is the primary measure of progress. Just as my father insisted every component of his machines be flawless before assembly, in software development each feature, user story, and technical element must function on its own and meet quality standards before integration. That discipline is what makes the final product robust, reliable, and truly valuable.

What surprised me most was how those workshop lessons returned years later in the most ordinary place – a Best Buy store. I didn't expect to find Agile hiding between TV manuals and remotes, but that's exactly what happened.

More than a decade after my formative experiences in my father's workshop, I moved to the U.S. and reconnected with two close friends, Akin and Femi. One weekend, Femi had just moved into a new apartment and needed a new TV, so the three of us headed to Best Buy to help him pick one out. It didn't take long to see the impact of their preliminary coaching as they approached the purchase. As we browsed through different brands – LG, Samsung, and others – we eventually found a model with all the specs he wanted.

At Best Buy, Femi kept flipping through the manual, scanning specs and features. Akin laughed and said, "*Forget the manual – just turn it on. Working software is the primary measure of progress.*"

That line stopped me cold. It was the first time I'd heard Agile language, and I didn't yet understand it. I asked, "What do you mean by 'working software is the primary measure of progress' and 'working software over comprehensive documentation'?"

They both laughed, realizing I hadn't been exposed to Agile yet. Still, the phrase struck me – it wasn't random talk; it sounded like a principle. And instantly, it reminded me of my father's workshop: don't obsess over appearances – make sure it truly works.

At the time, I was still managing projects using traditional methods – focused on scope, cost, and timelines, but not necessarily on adaptability or incremental delivery.

On the drive back home, I couldn't shake the curiosity. I asked again, "Seriously, what is Agile?" That's when they broke it down. Though, to be honest, I had already sneakily Googled it before they started explaining (lol).

They said Agile is a mindset. One centered on values like collaboration, adaptability, transparency, and delivering real, functional value incrementally. They explained how Agile helps reduce waste, improve team communication, and focus on what truly matters to customers. They were just learning Agile at the time too, but I could see the excitement in them – it was genuine, contagious.

But they didn't stop there.

Noticing my growing interest, Akin and Femi said, "*You need to meet Eddie.*"

To me, Eldee was a cultural icon in music. Now, they were telling me he had become an Agile Coach. That contrast intrigued me immediately.

When I finally met him, everything clicked. He spoke about Agile not just as a framework, but as a mindset – a way of thinking and leading. His depth of understanding and the way he connected values to real transformation drew me in. Over time, I chose him as my mentor, and that relationship shaped my path in profound ways.

Through Eddie, I didn't just learn the framework – I learned how to live it.

By the time I found myself working in an Agile environment, it felt like second nature. Having grown up in a setting that valued working components over superficial polish, I was able to help my software development team focus on delivering real value – working software that users could interact with, test, and rely on.

This mindset shift helped the team catch bugs early and ensure each component met quality standards before integration. It marked a transformation from a documentation-heavy approach to one that prioritized functional increments – a shift that aligned perfectly with Agile Principle #7.

I remember joining a team that had just started transitioning to Agile. They were so used to producing and sending documents to stakeholders that they spent more time writing and designing PowerPoints, Google Docs, and Word documents than actually developing. I understood their reasoning – stakeholders often appreciate documentation. But from experience, I knew they would prefer to see a working product over a polished stack of slides and files any day.

Bringing that perspective into the team gradually shifted their approach. They began to recognize the value in delivering something tangible – something that worked – something stakeholders could use and provide feedback on. It wasn't just about the software anymore; it was about building trust, improving communication, and fostering a culture of continuous improvement.

The principle that "working software is the primary measure of progress" goes beyond just code. It's about building stronger relationships with stakeholders, fostering confidence, and driving steady progress – not just in what we deliver, but how we deliver it. It's about evolution in our processes, our standards, and our relationships.

Reflecting on my journey, I now see how the lesson from my father's workshop – reinforced by Agile values, my friends, and my mentor – has become a guiding principle in both my career and my life. It's not just about delivering a product; it's about ensuring every step of the journey is anchored in value, quality, and true progress.

But this realization isn't unique to me. Many of us have been living these principles in different forms, often without realizing it. Whether it's a parent running a small shop, a teacher adapting lessons to meet students' needs, or a creative finding new ways to improve their craft – the essence of Agile is all around us. It's in the way we learn, adapt, and strive for continuous improvement in everything we do.

Agile isn't just a framework or a set of practices limited to software development; it's a mindset – a way of approaching life and work that prioritizes value, adaptability, and measurable progress.

So, as you read this, think about the areas in your own life where you're already applying these principles. You might be surprised to find that the Agile mindset has been part of your journey all along – just waiting to be recognized, embraced, and fully harnessed.

Takeaway for Readers:
Working software is the primary measure of progress.

Delivering real, working value, piece by piece, is what true progress looks like. Just as my father ensured each machine component was flawless before assembly, we must focus on building functional increments that serve a purpose. Agile reminds us that working software is the primary measure of progress, and that mindset helps teams stay anchored in what truly matters: value, quality, and usability.

Agile isn't just a framework – it's a way of thinking. Many of us have practiced its principles unknowingly, whether in a family business, a classroom, or a creative pursuit. It's not about tools or buzzwords; it's about adaptability, continuous improvement, and strong stakeholder relationships. Progress, in this context, is not only about what we deliver, but how we evolve throughout the journey.

Chapter 8
The Rhythm That Lasts: The Power of Sustainable Pace

Pace. It's the difference between a sprinter who burns out after 100 meters and a marathoner who crosses the finish line strongly. In Agile, pace isn't just about speed – it's about rhythm, endurance, and the ability to keep going without breaking. Anyone can sprint for a while, but the real test is whether you can deliver value week after week, month after month, without exhausting the people making it happen. That's where the game changes.

That's the power of sustainable development – captured in Agile Principle #8: "Agile processes promote sustainable development. The sponsors, developers, and users should be able to maintain a constant pace indefinitely." It's about finding a rhythm that can be maintained without burning out anyone involved, delivering consistently, week after week, without sacrificing people, energy, or quality. It's the difference between delivering something once and delivering again and again, with the same quality, energy, and focus.

Do you remember what we explored back in Chapter 4? Here's a quick refresher. That chapter showed how alignment, shared goals, and mutual trust between sponsors and teams can accelerate value delivery. But what happens when that alignment is tested – when momentum turns into burnout? That's where sustainable development comes in. And that is exactly what this chapter is here to unpack.

Chapter 4 emphasized the power of collaboration – how sponsors and teams working closely can unlock better outcomes. This chapter takes that relationship a step further. It's not just about working together, it's about lasting together. Agile isn't built for short bursts of glory followed by long periods of exhaustion. It's about finding a rhythm that allows everyone, including sponsors, developers, and users to move forward at a sustainable pace.

The knowledge in this chapter will reinforce and build on what you learned in Chapter 4. In the long run, how we deliver is just as important as what we deliver.

This chapter will deepen your understanding – not just in terms of frameworks or workflows, but in the real moments where people are stretched and must choose between pushing harder or pacing smarter. There are stories, even outside of Agile, that show us what it really means to find balance when the pressure is on.

Let's go on a side-quest into the world of music for a moment. I once followed the journey of an artist who was known for bringing raw energy to every show. His performances weren't just about hitting notes – they were an experience, made richer by the live band that traveled with him from city to city. Every performance was dynamic, real, and fully collaborative. But as the tour rolled on, something started to happen: burnout. Constant travel, non-stop rehearsals, and high-energy performances began to wear down not just the artist, but the entire crew. And the tour wasn't over – they still had more cities ahead.

Instead of pushing harder and risking a total collapse, they made a sustainable shift. On some nights, they replaced certain live band segments with a DJ playing the track, while the artist sang along or even mimed parts of the performance. This gave the band space to breathe, the artist time to reset, and even the audience – who, in our Agile context, could be seen as the users – a chance to relax and enjoy without the constant high-energy pace. On other nights, they would carefully restructure the setlist, inserting slow, soulful songs in the middle of high-energy sets to create a natural break for everyone. These weren't shortcuts; they were smart, strategic pauses that allowed the team to last together – proving that sometimes, the key to keeping the music alive is knowing exactly when to let it breathe.

In Agile terms, this is like temporarily reducing the team's workload so they can recover without stopping delivery altogether. It's alternating between high-effort features and smaller, low-effort tasks to keep progress moving without draining the team. Strategic adjustments like this are what make sustainable pace possible – ensuring value is delivered consistently and the journey isn't cut short by burnout.

I carry that same mindset into my work as an Agile lead. Think of the touring artist I mentioned earlier – by mid-tour, he still had more cities ahead, just like a team staring down a packed backlog or looming deadlines. When I sense the pace is accelerating – competing priorities, back-to-back meetings, and mounting deliverables – I don't wait for burnout to set in. Instead, I intentionally schedule downtime for the team. Sometimes it's a lively game of Kahoot; other times, a fun round of Wheel of Names with light-hearted banter. These sessions are sacred: no work talk, no JIRA tabs, no deliverables – just space to reset and recharge, so the team returns with fresh energy – recharged, sharper, and ready to keep delivering value.

This doesn't mean people aren't showing up – it means they're recharging so they can show up better. It's like the band on tour inserting DJ segments, slower-tempo songs, or even calling a quick "*let's take five*" or "*let's take ten*," giving everyone a moment to stretch, grab a drink, or simply catch their breath without losing momentum. In many modern offices, you'll find the same idea woven into the culture – game rooms, gyms, or breakout spaces meant to break up the monotony and sustain productivity. It also extends to vacations, because we all know that stepping away helps us come back stronger – recharged, sharper, and ready to keep delivering value.

In some Asian countries, workplace culture even supports structured downtime during the day. In parts of China, it's common for employees to take a short nap after lunch – a practice known to boost focus and creativity. In Japan, there's a cultural norm called 'inemuri', where briefly dozing off at your desk isn't frowned upon but seen as a sign of dedication and effort.

In short, you don't need a workstation full of deliverables to make progress. Sometimes, taking time to breathe, reset, and restore focus is the smartest move a team can make. The result? A sharper, more engaged team that can sustain performance – not just meet the next deadline, but keep delivering strong beyond it.

Of course, there will be moments when deadlines are pressing and the sponsors, team members, and even users agree to put in extra time, sometimes over a weekend or during a holiday, to keep the momentum alive. When this happens, it works best because everyone is on the same page. But this isn't just about alignment; it's about the energy, synergy, and shared commitment that allow the work to continue without breaking people in the process.

Just as a team can decide to lean in and push harder when needed, they can also decide together to step back and recharge. That decision is just as strategic as delivering on time. As a servant leader, I pay close attention to these moments – looking for opportunities to help the team protect their sustainable pace. Sometimes that means encouraging a break; other times, it means motivating them to rally and give a little extra. And when I say, "Team" I mean everyone involved – sponsors, developers, and users – because in Agile, we are all part of the same crew working toward a shared goal.

I've had experiences where sudden changes tested our ability to keep a sustainable pace. Once, a developer on my team had a family emergency and needed to step away. Naturally, this affected the team's dynamic – which is to be expected. Any time someone leaves or joins a team, there's usually some impact on how the team works together. But as the Agile lead, I make it my responsibility to balance things out so we can keep moving without losing momentum.

In this case, I asked the team who could step in to cover his work while he was away. Two team members immediately volunteered to take on his tasks. This happened because we had already built a culture of readiness – what I like to call "always keep water for drought". You never know when you'll need that preparation, but when you do, it can be the difference between slowing down and staying steady.

One way I foster this readiness is through pair programming and cross-training. It ensures that if someone has to step away unexpectedly, others are already familiar with their work and can pick it up seamlessly. While he was away, the rest of the team covered for him so well that no one outside the team would have known he was on emergency leave – well, maybe his timecard knew… and his direct manager, of course. But to everyone else, it was business as usual, and our deliverables stayed rock-solid.

By the time the developer returned – three weeks later, after resolving his family emergency – the outcome spoke for itself. The team was more focused, minds were sharper, and the energy felt lighter. The dynamic hadn't been lost. The team members who had stepped in to cover his work simply handed the responsibilities back, and everything continued as normal.

People came back to their usual roles refreshed and re-engaged, and our value delivery stayed sustainable – before he left, while he was gone, and after he returned. It wasn't forced; it was natural. That's because we had people on the team who understood that breaking the pace could harm our ability to deliver. We had already "kept water for drought," so when the moment came, they stepped up without hesitation.

And stepping up without hesitation isn't just about covering when someone has an emergency. It can be anything – helping a new team member get up to speed so the pace isn't lost, covering for someone on vacation, adapting during holiday periods, or even sustaining rapid releases to gain a competitive edge, like we discussed in Chapter 2, but this time with continuity in mind. Sometimes the situation calls for keeping features rolling out back-to-back during a critical season; other times, it's about adjusting to maintain flow through smaller, unexpected shifts. In every case, a truly Agile team must protect sustainability and pace, proving through action – not just words – that they are living Agile.

Going back to the band example, imagine the energy in the room when the drummer suddenly has to step away. The crowd is still buzzing, the lights are still on, and the show must go on. Because they've prepared, the band can seamlessly switch to a DJ for certain songs, even if that's not their usual style. Or they might strip it down and perform an acoustic set until the drummer returns. If the keyboard player is out sick, the guitarist can adjust and carry some of those melodies. The point is, the rhythm never stops. Sustainability and pace are what keep the music alive – and in Agile, they're what keep value flowing to sponsors and users, no matter what happens behind the scenes.

Whether it's a world tour or a software release, the goal is the same: to perform well over time, keeping the rhythm alive.

You see this same principle in a well-run restaurant kitchen. The head chef (sponsor) knows that on any given night, a sous chef or pastry chef (team members) might be unavailable. In a sustainable kitchen, this isn't a crisis because the work pace is already designed to be steady, not frantic. Staff are cross-trained – line cooks can step into prep work, and even servers understand enough about the process to help with plating in a pinch. This means the diners (users) still get their meals on time and at the same quality they expect – not because the team pulled off a last-minute save, but because the kitchen runs at a rhythm they can keep every night. Just like in Agile, this readiness and balanced pace don't happen by accident – they're built into the culture, so service continues smoothly, customers remain happy, and no one is run into the ground.

The same mindset shows up on a film production set. The producer (sponsor) is focused on the overall vision, the crew (team) brings that vision to life, and the audience (users) eagerly awaits the finished film. Film schedules can be intense, but sustainable productions pace themselves so cast and crew can perform at their best for weeks or months at a time. If the lighting operator can't make it one day, a cross-trained camera assistant can step in without throwing the schedule into chaos. If an actor is unavailable, the director might shoot from another angle or focus on different scenes. The key is that the schedule and workload are already designed to absorb these shifts without exhausting the crew. The audience still gets their premiere on time, and the producer's vision is delivered without burning people out.

This principle isn't limited to workplaces – it's present in everyday life, too. Think about the dynamic between parents, teachers, and students. The parents (sponsors) provide support and resources, the teachers (team) deliver the lessons, and the students (users) benefit from the learning experience. A healthy school year isn't a mad dash; it's paced so learning happens steadily from start to finish. When a teacher can't be in class, a substitute steps in – or the parents help keep learning on track at home. If a student needs extra help, both parents and teachers adjust their approach without overloading anyone. The goal isn't just to finish the syllabus – it's to keep a pace of learning that can be maintained all year, so everyone stays engaged, motivated, and capable of delivering their part.

For example, in one of the most popular frameworks within Agile – Scrum – a team will choose a sprint cadence of one, two, three, or four weeks based on what they're building, and then stick with it to maintain sustainability and pace. You don't see a Scrum team sprint for two weeks, switch to three, and then bounce back to two again – at least, I've never seen it. If it does happen, I'd love to hear about it, because chances are it would disrupt the team's rhythm and go against this Agile principle. The aim is to keep a steady beat in development, because that rhythm not only helps the team deliver value consistently, it builds a reputation for being strong, dependable, and trustworthy. A steady cadence keeps value flowing and prevents the kind of turbulence that can throw a team off course.

And while Scrum is just one example of an Agile framework, the idea of maintaining a constant pace applies across all Agile approaches. Whether you're working in Kanban, Extreme Programming, or a hybrid model, the goal remains the same: establish a delivery rhythm that can be sustained indefinitely, so value keeps flowing and the people delivering it remain energized.

All of these examples point to one thing: the ability to keep going at a pace that works for everyone involved. As a diner, I want to return to the same restaurant that respects my reservation and consistently delivers my food within a reliable window – say, 20 to 30 minutes after I'm seated. As a movie lover, I want to keep watching films from a studio that has proven it can release quality productions on a steady, predictable schedule – maybe every six months or once a year. As a parent, I want my child's learning pace to keep flowing without disruption, following a syllabus that's designed to be completed over the course of the school year without overwhelming anyone. And as an Agile team, I want to keep delivering value to my end users continuously by maintaining a consistent timebox cadence. This is one of the many ways to ensure delivery stays reliable and trusted – no matter what's happening behind the scenes – while also protecting the people doing the work. Users, like diners, moviegoers, and students, become part of the sustainability equation when they value and support a pace that can be maintained indefinitely. Spending our money, attention, feedback or energy with these providers is our contribution to helping that pace last.

Sometimes, the way this pace is maintained isn't visible to us, but it's happening. There are adjustments, substitutions, and quiet moments of teamwork – whether behind the scenes or right in front of us – that make it possible. And in Agile, just like in these everyday scenarios, the goal is the same: to keep a sustainable pace while working together, so that sponsors, teams, and users can all rely on the value being delivered consistently – not just once, but again and again, for as long as it takes to deliver the vision.

We often see someone's life fall apart and wonder how they manage to keep going. At other moments, we watch people stay at the top of their game, maintaining momentum year after year. In both cases, there's almost always something happening behind the scenes – choices, habits, and small resets that allow them to keep their rhythm. Whatever they're doing behind the scenes to stay afloat and keep moving forward, that's Agile Principle #8 in action – even if they don't realize it.

For some, it's taking a vacation, hitting the gym, watching a sports game, reading a book, going on a date, or picking up a new hobby. I once had a friend who decided to learn bartending – not because he wanted a career change, but because he needed a short break from the weight of everything else. That reset gave him the energy to come back stronger and keep going. On the flip side, I've seen people choose to push through for a while – maybe because a sibling's wedding was coming up, a cousin's graduation was around the corner, or a sports season was about to start – and they wanted to wrap up what they were doing before those moments arrived. One needed a break, the other needed to push harder. Both sustained themselves, but their pacing looked different. In the end, their goal was the same: to keep moving forward without burning out – adapting their approach to match their energy and capabilities. That's Agile Principle #8 in action, even if they didn't know they were living it.

With all the activities, scenarios, and examples mentioned above, you might pause for a moment and realize you've been applying this principle in your personal life without even knowing you were being Agile. Or perhaps you subconsciously knew you were Agile, but never connected those moments to this specific principle – or recognized the stage or situation it mirrors. Well, now you can. Consider this your official "aha" moment… and yes, you're welcome. (lol)

The same way individuals pace themselves in life is how Agile teams pace themselves in delivery – balancing rest and focused pushes. A sustainable pace means knowing when to slow down and when to push, so you can keep delivering value strong, steady, and effective for the long run.

Takeaway for Readers:
Agile processes promote sustainable development. The sponsors, developers, and users should be able to maintain a constant pace indefinitely.

Sustainable pace isn't about working slower – it's about working smarter. Balance energy and delivery, and you'll be able to keep delivering value consistently without burning yourself or your team out. Agile Principle #8 is like a marathon, not a sprint. Keep your rhythm steady, make time for recovery, and the finish line will always be within reach – no matter how far the journey.

Protecting the people doing the work protects the value being delivered. A sustainable pace keeps teams energized, engaged, and ready to deliver again tomorrow. Agile teams and individuals should know when to push and when to pause, so they can keep delivering strong for the long run. Whether in software, sports, music, or everyday life, lasting success comes from pacing yourself. Sustainable delivery is possible when rest and effort work in harmony.

Chapter 9
Beyond the Surface: Building for Today and Tomorrow

It was the early 2000s, and I was still a teenager. At that time, Nigeria had its own kind of "pandemic" – not a disease, but a craze. The lottery game known popularly as "Baba Ijebu" had spread like wildfire.

The owner of this lottery company is a man from Ijebu, a well-known city and one of the most influential tribes in southwest Nigeria. Because he comes from Ijebu, people started calling the lottery itself Baba Ijebu. In Yoruba culture, Baba means "father," and putting Baba in front of something is both a sign of respect and a playful nickname – especially for someone older, say in their 50s. And even among Nigerian guys in their younger age, Baba is sometimes used casually to greet one another with respect, especially when they don't know your name.

It's kind of like how you might call someone "Baba Georgia" if they're from Georgia, or "Baba Cali" if they're from California. Honestly, you can be Baba anything – Baba Chelsea, Baba Seahawks, Baba 49ers – once people know that's your thing.

That little nickname stuck, almost everyone knew about Baba Ijebu. Some played it openly, others in hiding to avoid judgment, but it had become part of daily conversations across the southwest of the country. For many, it was a dream of sudden fortune in a land where opportunities were scarce.

Two of my uncles were among those who played – openly and unapologetically. And one Saturday night, both of them hit it big. I still remember they had staked a "two direct" and a "three direct" across multiple tickets. That night, the numbers lined up, and their combined luck translated into a massive win.

Each walked away with around 6 million naira, which at the time was roughly $50,000. To put that in perspective: back then, the exchange rate hovered around 132–135 naira to the dollar. Compare that to today's 1,560 naira to a dollar, as of the time I'm revising this chapter in 2025, and you realize just how significant their winnings were.

That $50,000 win became the starting point for a story that would later teach me an unforgettable lesson about design, stability, and the foundation we choose to build upon. It's a lesson I only came to fully appreciate years later, when I encountered Agile principles and realized how clearly this memory reflected them. This moment gave me clarity on how Agile Principle #9 truly works in practice – the very essence of building with technical excellence and good design.

With their winnings in hand, both of my uncles made the same decision: they would build houses. Not just anywhere, but side by side, on two plots of land. At first glance, it looked like the beginning of two identical success stories. But as I watched their choices unfold – the materials they selected, the foundations they laid, and the way they approached the entire process – I began to notice something that would later remind me of Agile Principle #9.

Their winnings came around August, and both were determined to complete their houses before Christmas and New Year so they could proudly host friends for a double celebration – housewarming and holiday festivities. Fortunately, they already had land inherited from our grandfather, which made the decision to build quick and straightforward.

Due to the tight timeline, they both agreed that building bungalows was the best option. This way, they could complete the houses quickly. Both had the same idea and even worked with the same architect. Let's call them Uncle Jide and Uncle Sola.

But when it came to the details, their paths diverged. Uncle Sola asked the architect to include pillars at the corners where each room connected to a wall. Curious, Uncle Jide called him out during one of their design discussions.

"Why add extra pillars?" Uncle Jide asked. *"We only need the ones for doors and windows."*

Uncle Sola explained his reasoning: *"I'm thinking about the future. One day I might want to add another floor on top of this house. Instead of buying more land or spending more money later, I'd rather prepare for it now."*

The architect nodded in agreement with Uncle Sola's idea. But Uncle Jide shook his head. To him, this was unnecessary.

He was worried about two things: it might threaten the Christmas deadline, and it would be too expensive, especially with the rising cost of cement and iron needed for the extra concrete pillars.

When the quotations came back, Uncle Sola's estimate was about 30% higher than Uncle Jide's due to the additional pillars. In Uncle Jide's mind, the house just needed to be ready for December, nothing more. But for Uncle Sola, the vision was long-term, not just a holiday party.

Uncle Sola had also done his refinement and research, speaking directly with the contractor. He was reassured that, even with the extra pillars, the house could still be completed on time – before Christmas. With that guarantee, he was comfortable investing more for a stronger foundation.

In the end, both houses were completed on schedule. Uncle Jide's house was finished about two weeks earlier than Uncle Sola's, but by Christmas, both families were able to host their friends and celebrate, just as they had planned.

From the outside, the two homes looked almost identical – same layout, same design, same finishing touches. The only difference was hidden within the walls: Uncle Sola's house carried extra pillars at the corners of each room, while Uncle Jide's did not. That small detail was the only thing that set their homes apart, but it carried a lesson I wouldn't fully understand until much later.

Fast forward seven years later. A popular market had been relocated to our town, and a new tertiary institution was opened as well. This brought a wave of people – traders, business owners, students – and soon, housing scarcity became a major issue. Demand was so high that whenever a new house development began, tenants would sometimes pay rent in advance even before the house was completed, especially once it reached the finishing stage.

By this time, both uncles had long run out of their lottery money (I bet we all knew that would happen – (lol)). Life was back to normal, and though they still tried their luck here and there, fortune didn't smile on them again. They eventually decided to relocate to Europe. But before leaving, they faced a big decision: what to do with their houses.

They didn't want to leave the homes behind, so selling seemed like the best option. Land and old houses had become hot cakes because of the new developments in town. In fact, many buyers would purchase older homes just to demolish them and rebuild commercial properties from scratch.

A developer came along and offered both uncles the same price for their houses, with the assumption that both would be torn down and replaced with new commercial buildings. Uncle Jide was excited and ready to accept the offer immediately. But Uncle Sola paused.

He believed his house had more to offer. He shared his architectural plans with the developer, explaining that instead of demolishing everything, they could build a decking (an additional floor) on top of his existing structure. The pillars he had invested in years earlier made that possible.

The developer was impressed – so much so that he increased his offer by 43% more than what he had offered Uncle Jide. In the end, Uncle Jide's house was demolished to the ground and replaced with a brand-new commercial building, while Uncle Sola's house was expanded upwards, the new floor resting on the pillars he had built into the design years before.

At the time, it was just a family story I admired from the sidelines. But years later, when I began working in Agile environments, I realized this story wasn't just about bricks, pillars, or Christmas parties – it was about the very choices teams make in software projects. I know you're probably wondering what all of this has to do with Agile Principle #9, which states: "Continuous attention to technical excellence and good design enhances agility.

At first glance, both houses seemed like identical successes. By Christmas, both uncles had hosted their friends, and from the outside, no one could tell the difference. This is often how projects feel when a team hits a deadline: the product demo looks smooth, the go-live is celebrated, and from the surface, everything seems fine. But just like the houses, what people don't see are the invisible design choices made beneath the surface – the foundation that determines whether the system can evolve or eventually collapse.

In Uncle Jide's case, the focus was purely on speed and cost. He wanted to move in as quickly as possible, and he succeeded – finishing two weeks earlier and spending less money. But speed without foresight is fragile. His house had no capacity to adapt to change. It was built for that moment in December, and nothing more. This mirrors what happens in many projects when stakeholders push for a release date at all costs. The frontend looks good enough to impress, but the foundation is left fragile, rushed, or incomplete.

Uncle Sola, on the other hand, invested in what couldn't be seen. His extra pillars were like solid backend design or clean architecture in a software project. At first, it seemed unnecessary. It cost 30% more, and no one at the Christmas party even noticed the difference. But those invisible choices gave his house something Uncle Jide's house lacked: the capacity to adapt. Uncle Jide's home had speed, but it lacked good design – and without good design, there can be no true agility.

Years later, when demand in the town exploded and developers were buying houses, the difference became undeniable. Uncle Jide's house was demolished completely – the equivalent of rewriting a poorly designed system from scratch because it couldn't scale. Uncle Sola's house, on the other hand, was extended. His upfront investment paid off when his home was valued forty-three per cent higher. This is what technical excellence looks like in action: it may not shine in the demo, but it creates business value when change inevitably comes.

This is exactly what happens in projects too. Stakeholders often demand a go-live to meet market pressures or deadlines, but they rarely care how the foundation is built. Their only goal is to meet the target. Teams that cave to this pressure and skip quality create technical debt – systems that work today but collapse tomorrow. It feels cheaper and faster in the moment, but it always costs more later.

Agile Principle #9 is a reminder that technical excellence isn't just engineering pride – it's business wisdom. A strong backend may require extra effort initially, but it keeps you adaptable when requirements shift, markets change, or growth demands expansion. It's the difference between tearing everything down to start over or building on what you already have.

When we focus only on the visible – the frontend, the demo, the immediate deadline – we get Uncle Jide's house: temporary success but no future flexibility. When we balance deadlines with thoughtful design, we get Uncle Sola's house: resilient, adaptable, and ultimately more valuable.

That lesson didn't just stay with me as a childhood memory – I carried it into my professional life. And sure enough, I watched the exact same pattern play out years later in a high-stakes project. Stories like my uncles' houses aren't just family memories; I've seen the same pattern play out in my professional life as well. In software development, the pressure to deliver quickly often pushes teams to focus only on the visible – the "Christmas party" equivalent of a product demo or go-live date. But just like with Uncle Jide and Uncle Sola, it's the unseen design choices beneath the surface that determine whether the system can adapt when the real test comes. I experienced this firsthand while preparing for a Black Friday launch with one of the teams I used to work with.

It was early October, and an e-commerce company was gearing up for the biggest sales day of the year: Black Friday. The engineering team had been working on a real-time sales dashboard to track critical metrics like orders per minute (OPM), revenue, and system health. On the surface, everything looked good. The dashboard handled test data smoothly, and leadership was impressed by early demos.

But the truth was hidden beneath the surface. One engineer had raised a concern months earlier: the way the data queries were written worked fine for small volumes but would be dangerously inefficient under the massive traffic expected during Black Friday. The team knew this, and I also stepped in to emphasize the engineer's concern, making sure they understood the consequences of ignoring it. I warned that what looked fine now could cost us dearly later. But under pressure to deliver something quickly for leadership, the decision was made to push the concern aside. "We'll optimize later," they said.

When the dashboard was connected to real production traffic in a trial run, the cracks showed immediately. The system lagged badly, unable to keep up with the load. Suddenly, the shortcut couldn't be ignored. With only three weeks before Black Friday, the entire data pipeline had to be redesigned. What should have been a quiet period of refinement turned into nights, weekends, and firefighting. Features that had been planned for the release were abandoned just to make sure the dashboard could function at a basic level.

The parallel to Uncle Jide's house is clear: the dashboard looked complete on the surface, but because the foundation – the query design – was weak, it couldn't adapt to the demands placed on it. The team had traded real agility for the illusion of speed.

Now imagine if Principle #9 had guided the work from the very beginning. Taking the time to design for scale, write efficient and maintainable queries, and actually listen to the engineer's warning – and my own persuasion – would have required an early investment. It might have slowed early demos, yes. But by the time Black Friday arrived, the system would have been ready, tested, and reliable – no late nights, no firefighting, no heroics required.

The lesson is simple but powerful: speed without quality isn't real speed – it's borrowing trouble from the future. Poor quality today becomes technical debt tomorrow. When you cut corners – skipping tests, ignoring refactoring, piling on quick fixes – your system may work in the moment, but it becomes fragile and messy.

Technical excellence isn't about doing everything at once; it's about creating the capacity to adapt when it matters most. Just as Uncle Sola's extra pillars gave his house long-term value, solid backend design would have given the Black Friday dashboard the stability to support the business when it was needed most. Well-designed, high-quality systems are flexible: they let you add features, scale, or make changes quickly and safely, without tearing everything down.

Think of it like keeping your kitchen clean while you cook. If you wash dishes, wipe counters, and organize ingredients as you go, you can prepare multiple meals smoothly. But if you pile up a mountain of dirty plates and clutter until the end, the kitchen becomes slow, chaotic, and stressful to work in. Technical excellence works the same way: small, consistent attention prevents a mess that overwhelms you later.

Or picture packing for a long trip with versatile clothing. If you bring items that mix and match, you can adapt to different weather, events, and unexpected plans without stress. But if you pack only flashy outfits for the first few days, you'll quickly run out of options and struggle later. In software, design for adaptability is like versatile clothing – it may not impress immediately, but it saves you when circumstances change.

City planning gives another clear example. A town that builds roads, power lines, and water systems with future expansion in mind will grow smoothly as new neighborhoods appear. But a city that builds only for today faces gridlock, bottlenecks, and costly rework when growth inevitably arrives. In the same way, software systems with a solid design foundation scale gracefully, while rushed shortcuts collapse under pressure.

You might have come across other examples to the ones I've shared here, and that's the very point of this book – to unlock what you may not notice but is right in front of you. These scenarios aren't about perfection; they're about opening your eyes to a way of seeing. Maybe your own story mirrors this principle more closely than mine. That's the beauty of Agile: it isn't about flawless execution, it's about continuous learning and recognizing how these principles show up in our everyday lives – because Agile is, quite literally, in plain sight.

Takeaway for Readers:
Continuous attention to technical excellence and good design enhances agility.

Agile isn't about perfection; it's about awareness and continuous learning. Look closely, and you'll find that principles like this show up not only in projects, but in everyday life. Just as Uncle Sola's house sold for more, well-designed systems deliver greater long-term returns than shortcuts ever will.

Technical debt is like building without pillars: it may feel faster and cheaper at the moment, but sooner or later the cost of rework will be greater than the cost of doing it right the first time. True agility doesn't come from rushing to meet deadlines – it comes from balancing delivery speed with design excellence, so systems remain adaptable when the market shifts.

Short-term wins can look impressive, but without solid design they crumble under future demands. Real agility is built for both today and tomorrow. And while technical excellence is often invisible at first, it reveals its value the moment change or pressure arrives. That's when good design proves its worth.

Chapter 10
Simplicity Isn't Laziness: It's Clarity & Focus

There's a special kind of energy when a team starts a brand-new product. Conversations overlap, ideas spark, and everyone believes their suggestion is the missing piece. That was exactly the atmosphere when we kicked off one of the e-commerce projects. Excitement was high, ideas were flying in from every direction, and the energy in the room was contagious.

On this project, I had the privilege of working with one of the most brilliant development teams I've ever met – smart, creative, and fearless. They weren't truly Agile yet but collaborating with them gave me the chance to coach, to challenge assumptions, and to guide them through mindset shifts. This new e-commerce initiative opened the door to uncovering many missed opportunities in how they approached agility, and it became a real proving ground for change. With both internal stakeholders and external partners involved, the project carried enormous potential – but also the familiar risk of drowning in opinions and documents.

A week earlier, we had held an introductory meeting. Nothing fancy – just a chance to bring the key players into the same room: stakeholders, subject matter experts, and the core team. The agenda was simple – discuss the problem statement, sketch possible approaches, and identify the stakeholders who would play major roles. On the surface, it was a standard kickoff. But even in that short session, I could sense how easily conversations could spiral into complexity if we weren't careful.

This kind of initial conversation isn't unique to software development. It happens in everyday life too. Think about when a couple first meets with a wedding planner: ideas rush in about venues, menus, flowers, and music long before the date is even locked down. Or when a family sits with a realtor for the first time – everyone chimes in with dream features, from a pool to a modern kitchen to a bigger backyard. The same thing happens when parents talk with their child about college; every voice adds suggestions, from majors to locations to scholarships. These conversations are filled with passion and possibility, but they can quickly become overwhelming if not anchored to the essentials.

And so it goes in life, business, or product development. Stakeholders will always want a long list of features, and teams are often tempted to add even more – based on what they think consumers might like or want. The energy of beginnings carries promise, but it also carries the risk of too much, too soon.

Leadership had asked for a simple overview – not a thesis – so they could understand how the frontend experience would shape up for customers. Of course, sometimes they say this but don't always mean it – *wink*. A senior UI/UX designer, Jasmine, was nominated to pull the story together. She was talented – no question about it. She knew design systems, customer journeys, and user flows like the back of her hand.

From that very first meeting, I could already sense risk and uncertainty. So, I planned to connect with Jas before the next big session, since she was responsible for presenting the frontend design to the group. And when I say "The group," I mean the leadership – stakeholders, SMEs, and the core team members all in one room.

With that many eyes and expectations, I knew one thing: if she was ready, then we were ready. Her clarity was the foundation for everything else. The next meeting was only a few days away, and my goal was simple – check in, align, and make sure we weren't about to drown in unnecessary detail.

As I was planning to reach out to her, boom – she caught me off guard and reached out first.

"Hey Adewale, when is the next meeting again? It's in two days, right?" she asked. Then she quickly added, *"I know it's in two days but just wanted to confirm with you."*

I smiled and replied, "Yes, it's in two days." Then I followed up, "What's up?"

She asked if she could get a quick meeting with me later. She wanted to have a second look at what she planned to share with the leadership. I couldn't resist joking:

"You know I'm not technical enough to understand whatever you're about to present – or make sense of your Figma."

She laughed and replied, *"Well, you never know – you might end up being the end user."*

We both burst out laughing. Then she said, *"I'd like to show this to you."*

"Sure," I said. "We can meet later."

And just like that, we agreed to connect before the big session.

Later that afternoon, we found a quiet corner and she pulled up her laptop. As the screen lit up, I noticed her Figma tabs and a massive presentation file already open. She gave me that excited smile, the kind that says, "I've been working on this nonstop."

"*Okay*," she said, "*let me walk you through what I plan to present.*"

Slide after slide started rolling. Detailed wireframes. Flow diagrams of every possible user journey. Variations of checkout pages, multiple color palettes, dropdown behaviors, even placeholder animations. By slide ten, I could see where this was heading. By slide twenty, I realized she was preparing to take the leadership on a tour of every single possibility – not just the essentials.

I let her finish before speaking, because I could see the pride in her work. She had poured hours into this. When she finally paused, I looked at her and began with a compliment.

"This is impressive," I said. "But let me ask you one question: if you had only three slides to explain to leadership how a customer would complete a checkout in the first release, what would you keep?"

The truth was, in my mind I was thinking five slides would be fair. But I deliberately said three – just to challenge her thinking, to force simplicity, to make her strip everything down to its absolute core.

She froze for a second, then smiled slowly. "*Three slides? That's impossible.*"

I grinned. "It's not impossible – it's simple. You can do this, Jas."

She raised an eyebrow.

"You're designing for clarity, not for volume," I continued. "The leadership doesn't need fifty slides of possibilities; they need three slides that prove customers can buy something without friction. Everything else can wait."

She looked back at her deck, then looked at me again. "*So you're saying less is more?*"

"Exactly," I said. "Less isn't clutter – it's clarity. It's what will keep us from drowning in unnecessary detail."

We both sat in silence for a moment, staring at the mountain of slides. Then she laughed.

"*Alright, Adewale – you win. But how about four slides? I'll find the four that matter, and if I need to modify them later, I will,*" she said with a playful grin.

I nodded. "Go for it, Jas."

One of the best things about Agile is the space it creates for flexibility and negotiation. This will always happen when you're working with a team – any team – whether it's in a professional setting or in our personal lives. You could see it right there in how Jas and I settled on the number of slides. It wasn't about winning or losing; it was about aligning on what mattered most and moving forward together.

Jas asked if she could send the slides to me for a quick review prior to the meeting. I declined and told her, "I trust your judgment, no doubt. I'm not here to direct you – just sharing my two cents. Just keep in mind: complexity looks impressive, but simplicity delivers results." She smiled and said, "*I got you, Adewale.*"

On the day of the meeting, everyone was ready in the conference room and we were about to commence. I did the introduction and braced myself for questions from a few stakeholders – the ones who always expect to see every possible feature crammed into the deck. I knew those questions would come, so I was prepared just in case the team didn't have an answer. From past conversations, the team already understood one of my favorite reminders: every 'yes' to something unimportant is a silent 'no' to what truly matters. That gave me confidence they'd know when to say "no" to features that didn't matter.

Then Jas connected her laptop to the big screen. As she walked through the agenda, I could almost feel the room shift – especially from the stakeholders who had been expecting twenty or thirty slides. Instead, Jas had just four, aside from the basics like the agenda, a questions slide, and an appendix. Each slide was focused, clear, and designed to spark meaningful conversation, dialogue, and negotiation if needed. The surprise was written all over their faces.

The first slide came up on the big screen, and Jas walked the room through the core outcome: browse, add to cart, and complete checkout with one payment option. Simple. Direct. Achievable.

A couple of eyebrows raised. One stakeholder leaned forward and whispered to the person next to him. By the second slide – a clean wireframe flow showing the end-to-end path – hands started to go up.

"*Wait, is this it?*" one stakeholder finally asked.

"*Yes,*" Jas replied calmly, "*this is the flow we're focusing on for the first release. It's the backbone that makes everything else possible.*"

Another voice chimed in: "*But where's the loyalty program? Where are the discounts? What about multi-item carts?*"

Jas paused for a moment, and that's when I stepped in.

"The goal for us was never about showing how much workload we could take on. It was about zeroing in on what truly mattered. With the timeline we had, the smartest move was to prioritize the must-haves – the essentials that would deliver value right away. The nice-to-haves could always come later, layered in once the foundation was strong.

True progress isn't measured by how much we build, but by how little we waste. Let's keep the focus on the first release – especially with the short timeline we have right now. Everything else can be marked as out of scope for now, while this core flow stays in scope on Jas's deck. That way, we make real progress first and add the extras later."

The stakeholder who had raised the concern leaned back, thought for a moment, and finally nodded. "*Okay…that makes sense.*"

The director at the table, who had been quietly watching, leaned forward and added, "*This is exactly what we need. Simple, clear, focused. If we can get this working in the first release, then we can layer in the rest.*"

I watched the tension in the room melt away. What could have spiraled into twenty features or twenty slides instead became alignment around one clear outcome. Jas had delivered exactly what leadership asked for, even if they didn't realize they meant it when they first said "simple overview." It had been delivered.

The agreement around four slides wasn't just a tactical win; it revealed a deeper shift. This wasn't about decks anymore – it was about how the team thought, how they prioritized, and how they defended simplicity in the face of pressure.

Walking out of that room, I could see something had clicked – not just for leadership, but for Jas and the team. That meeting wasn't just about slides; it was about mindset. And it showed them that the art of simplicity wasn't about delivering more, but about ensuring that less – when focused on what truly matters – delivers the most value. They often built massive slide decks at kickoffs. But those decks only left them overcommitted to work they could never deliver. This new approach shifted their mindset: the team began to see that success meant focusing on what matters first, not trying to cover everything that matters all at once.

I also knew that one of their biggest challenges had always been saying no to stakeholders who demanded too much, too soon. With my guidance, they started learning how to respond with confidence – how to explain priorities and draw the line in a respectful but firm way. They came to realize that simplicity demands courage: the courage to say "No" when something doesn't matter right now, and the wisdom to say "Yes" when it can wait.

That shift was powerful – but it wasn't new. It echoed something we had already uncovered earlier in this journey. If I can take you back to Chapter 7, we established a simple truth: working software is the primary measure of progress. Chapter 10 takes it further – showing that we get there faster when we ruthlessly simplify.

One pivot – from twenty slides to four – changed the project's trajectory. The team shipped a thin, working checkout flow ahead of schedule, then layered complexity only when it paid for itself. What used to be a debate about design possibilities in the past between the team and the stakeholders became a cadence of real progress: demo, learn, adjust, extend.

And everyone learned something important: simplicity isn't doing less work; it's choosing the right work. Simplicity is not anti-design. It's anti-waste. The design that matters most is the one that lets a real customer act. When you can show the path – from Browse to Add to Cart to Checkout – on one screen and one story, you are close to Chapter 7's promise: progress you can experience, not just describe.

That is the art of maximizing the work not done. Not because we're lazy, but because we're serious about outcomes. The shortest path to value is almost always a simpler path. When we honor that, simplicity becomes more than a project principle – it becomes a mindset for life itself. And that's important, because simplicity doesn't just belong in Agile rooms or design decks. It shows up everywhere. This truth showed up again in my personal life – at a wedding where I was the best man. During the preparation and planning phase, we talked to multiple vendors and what I realized was this: it was either we were asking for too much, or the event planning vendors were trying to add too much during the preliminary conversations.

We wanted everything – big cake, DJ songs, decoration colors, dresses, hall, type of food, and so on. The vendors, on the other hand, often piled on even more – sometimes tailoring our needs to suit their preferences, or adding services that would benefit them more than us. After several conversations that led nowhere, I pulled my friend aside and asked him a simple question: What's the most important thing we need – without which the wedding wouldn't even hold?

Once we identified that, we tailored the same approach with every vendor. First, solve for the essentials. Then, if resources allowed, we could add the nice-to-haves. That single shift gave us clarity, reduced stress, and ultimately made the wedding a success.

We simplified what mattered most before thinking about everything else. And that experience confirmed something deeper: this pattern isn't limited to software or even weddings. It's the same dynamic you'll find when buying a house, choosing a college, or setting yearly goals. Whenever possibilities pile up, simplicity is the tool that cuts through the noise and brings clarity.

As Agile Principle #10 states: "Simplicity – the art of maximizing the amount of work not done – is essential." Because in Agile and in life, simplicity is not laziness – it is focus, discipline, and wisdom.

Think about it: in our day-to-day lives, when our plans start to look like a bloated backlog, it's rarely a sign of innovation. More often, it's a sign of distraction. Impressive complexity fades fast, but focused simplicity lasts.

And just like Jas with her four slides, and my friend's wedding, I've learned the same truth: simplicity is universal. Whether you're planning a wedding, launching an e-commerce product, setting monthly or yearly goals, buying a house, or even relocating, the discipline of focusing on what matters most first will always bring better outcomes than trying to satisfy every possible want at once. Agile Principle #10 reminds us that maximizing the work not done is not just a technique – it's a mindset. It frees us to deliver value sooner, with less waste, and with the kind of clarity that everyone can rally behind.

"Simplicity is not about doing less – it's about doing what matters most, first."

Takeaway for Readers:
Simplicity – The art of maximizing the amount of work not done – is essential.

Simplicity always wins. Whether it's an Agile, a wedding plan, or everyday life, the discipline of focusing on what matters most first produces better outcomes. Simplicity isn't laziness – it's clarity. It's what frees us from clutter, stress, and distractions so progress feels clear and achievable.

The art of maximizing work not done is the art of maximizing clarity. Less – when it's the right less – creates the most value. More features don't equal more value; sometimes, more is just noise. Every "yes" to something unimportant is a silent "no" to what matters. True leadership is shown in the courage to simplify: to protect the essentials, to say no when it counts, and to reserve time and resources for what really moves the needle.

Complexity often looks impressive, but simplicity delivers results people can experience and celebrate. When we strip away noise, progress accelerates. We deliver sooner, with less waste, and with clarity that unites teams and satisfies customers. Simplicity isn't just an Agile principle – it's a universal truth for leaders, teams, and life itself.

Chapter 11
Seeds of Trust: Trees of Self-Organization

Across the street from where I once lived in Sacramento, California, USA, there was a small Indian grocery store. From the outside, it looked like any other neighborhood shop, but once you stepped in, it told a different story. The first thing you noticed was the warmth – the children of the owner, two girls and a boy, greeting every customer with a smile that stuck with you. It wasn't the kind of scripted politeness you might find in a chain store. No, this was genuine, as if you were walking into their extended home – and as I would later come to realize, it revealed something deeper about how the best teams organize themselves.

What struck me most was how little the father, the owner of the store, seemed to involve himself in the day-to-day operations. Sometimes he was nowhere to be found. I had never once seen their mother in the store; perhaps she was the anchor at home. But in that grocery store, the kids ran the show. They stocked shelves, arranged goods neatly, loaded up the freezers, handled deliveries, and even managed the shipping. Their father trusted them enough to let them organize the entire flow of the business without his constant presence.

At first glance, it might have looked like neglect, but in reality, it was the opposite – it was trust. The father had built an environment where his children could not only contribute but also self-organize. They didn't need him hovering, barking instructions, or managing every detail. Instead, each child naturally gravitated toward roles that matched their strengths and the energy they carried that day – one greeting customers at the counter, another arranging items on the shelves, and the third ensuring deliveries were completed on time. Nothing was forced; everything flowed.

The children weren't just completing chores; they were shaping how the store operated day by day. Every decision – where to place goods, how to arrange shelves, or who would handle deliveries – became part of a living design. In organizations, it's the same: self-organizing teams don't just "Do the work." They create the systems, workflows, and designs that leadership alone could never imagine. That's why self-organizing teams do more than manage tasks – they shape the very architecture of success.

There was no enforcement of requirements from their father, no checklist pinned to a wall, no design spelled out on a board for them to follow. The best "Architecture" for running that store did not come from a manual or a strict job description. It emerged from the children themselves, working together, adapting in the moment, and supporting one another.

One day, I noticed something unusual. The middle child, Kabir, was nowhere to be found in the store. This wasn't the first time I had seen him missing – in fact, it was about the third or fourth time. Out of curiosity, I asked one of his siblings, "Where's Kabir?" Without hesitation, they replied, *"Oh, he's in the next city overseeing our new store."*

I was taken aback. "Wait a minute," I said, "Kabir is going to be running the shop?" The youngest sibling answered firmly, with no inch of doubt in her voice: *"Yes."* At that time, Kabir was only around 19 years old.

Still curious, I asked, "So your mom is going to stay with him, right?" The answer surprised me even more. *"No,"* she said with calm certainty. *"He's the one managing the new store, but we hired a few people to support him."* Her tone carried no hesitation. This wasn't just about trust anymore – it was about recognition and reward. Kabir and his siblings had proven themselves as capable, self-organizing individuals. Their father's decision to let Kabir run a store of his own was the ultimate sign of confidence in what they had already demonstrated.

I later learned that their father only visited the new store once or twice a week, and only if it was truly necessary. In other words, he wasn't standing over Kabir's shoulder or micromanaging his every move. He had entrusted his son with ownership, responsibility, and freedom. Kabir had earned that by showing initiative, reliability, and the ability to self-organize alongside his siblings in the original store.

About five months later, I happened to be in the city where their new store was located. Even though I believed what I had heard, I wanted to see it for myself – to confirm how things really played out when the responsibility rested on Kabir's shoulders. When I walked in, Kabir greeted me with surprise, smiling because he knew me well. I found him in the middle of redesigning one of the store shelves to make space for new items, almost like he was giving the store its own fresh identity.

In many businesses, this type of change would have required a manager's approval, a video call with a supervisor, or direct instructions from the owner. But not here. Kabir was overseeing and executing it entirely on his own, working with the trust his father had placed in him. That didn't mean there were no conversations at home between father and son – of course there were. But in this store, Kabir called the shots. He decided when changes were needed, when finances should be reviewed, and when adjustments to branding or operations made sense. He wasn't shadowed, second-guessed, or doubted. He earned the space to lead.

That is what self-organization looks like: not chaos, not absence of leadership, but the freedom to make decisions responsibly and confidently. Kabir had the space to try, to adjust, and to learn, just like his siblings back at the original store. He wasn't simply running tasks; he was shaping the way the store operated.

What played out in that small family business mirrors exactly what happens in high-performing teams.

This is Agile Principle #11 in action: the best architectures, requirements, and designs emerge from self-organizing teams. The grocery store wasn't thriving because of the father's control. It thrived because he created the space for his kids to step in, figure things out, and make decisions as a unit. Their teamwork, not his oversight, was what gave structure and life to that small business.

In Agile teams, the same dynamic applies. Leaders can set direction, provide vision, and create an enabling environment. But it is the team itself that decides how to approach challenges, distribute responsibilities, and solve problems. Just like those kids in the store, Agile teams are at their best when given both the freedom and the trust to self-organize. The result? Solutions that are not only effective but also sustainable, because they come from those closest to the work.

Think about how each child in the store naturally gravitated toward different responsibilities. One was at the counter greeting customers, another was arranging items neatly on shelves, while another kept an eye on deliveries and stocking the refrigerators. None of this was written down in a manual or handed out as a strict assignment. They simply knew what needed to be done and took action. In the same way, a team that is trusted to self-organize doesn't wait for every instruction to come from above.

Work gets picked up, responsibilities shift, and progress happens because the team understands the goal and collaborates to achieve it.

The father, in this picture, represents leadership or stakeholders. His role was not to hover over every detail, but to set the environment and provide direction – much like leaders do in an organization. By choosing trust over control, he empowered his children to take ownership. This parallels how leadership in a healthy team environment provides vision and resources but allows the team itself to decide how best to deliver. The best designs and decisions emerge from the people doing the work, not from someone dictating each step from a distance.

Kabir's move to oversee the new store is a perfect example of how teams evolve and scale. At first, all the children worked together in one location, learning how to collaborate and manage the flow of the business. Over time, their self-organization matured to the point where they could extend that model beyond the walls of the original shop. Kabir took the principles of teamwork, ownership, and adaptability and applied them in a new context – much like how teams, when they grow in capability and trust, can scale their practices to new initiatives or product lines. This isn't just replication; it's evolution.

Another important aspect is how decisions were handled. At the new store, Kabir wasn't waiting for a phone call to ask permission for every little change. When he decided to redesign a shelf to accommodate different products, he simply acted. That didn't mean his father was absent; conversations about finances and strategy still happened. But in the moment-to-moment operations, Kabir had the freedom to experiment, learn, and adapt. In teams, this is critical. Self-organization thrives when members have both the responsibility and the authority to make decisions within their scope of work.

Even the dynamic between the siblings mirrors how teams balance responsibilities. On some days, one child might be better suited to handle customer interactions, while another might focus on logistics. This fluidity allowed the store to run smoothly without rigid assignments. Teams in the workplace mirror this when they shift roles based on context, skill sets, and immediate needs. What matters is not who owns the title, but how the group works together to keep momentum and value flowing.

Lastly, the father's choice to only step in when necessary highlights a critical point: oversight should never become overbearing. His weekly visits were not to micromanage, but to ensure that things were on track and to offer support if needed. In organizations, the same principle applies. Leaders provide checks and guidance, but the day-to-day success comes from the people closest to the work, trusted to organize themselves.

This grocery store story is more than a family business anecdote. It is a living example of how self-organization creates resilience, adaptability, and growth. When individuals are trusted to own their part of the whole, and when teams are given freedom to shape how they work, the results are far stronger than anything that could be written in a manual. That's why Agile Principle #11 resonates: the best architectures, requirements, and designs emerge from self-organizing teams.

Back in Chapter 5, we explored how projects thrive when built around motivated individuals, and how trust is the foundation for unlocking their potential. Many of you will remember the story of Jacob, the stakeholder who initially struggled to let go of control. His constant micromanagement drained the team's energy and limited their ability to be creative. It wasn't that Jacob lacked good intentions; he simply believed the best way to achieve results was to stay involved in every decision. But the opposite happened – the more he pressed, the less ownership the team felt.

The turning point came when Jacob finally stepped back. Once he trusted the team to organize themselves, the energy shifted. Decisions were made faster, creativity started flowing, and the team began producing results that exceeded expectations. By stepping back, Jacob didn't lose control – instead, he gained something far greater: a team that was motivated, engaged, and capable of delivering value on its own.

Chapter 11 builds directly on that lesson. In the story of Kabir and his siblings, we see the same principle play out in a very different setting. Their father, like Jacob, was in a position of authority. But unlike Jacob at the start, Kabir's father understood the power of stepping back from the beginning. He didn't stand over his children's shoulders, dictating every move. He created the space for them to contribute, experiment, and grow. The result? A thriving business and children who were capable of running not just one store but scaling that model to another city.

The comparison between Jacob and Kabir's father is powerful for any organization. Jacob shows us the consequences of micromanagement: disengagement, frustration, and limited results. Kabir's father shows us the benefits of trust: ownership, innovation, and sustainable growth. Both leaders cared, but only one created an environment where the best "Architecture" could emerge naturally.

This reinforcement matters because Chapter 5 and Chapter 11 are two sides of the same coin. Chapter 5 is about trusting motivated individuals. Chapter 11 is about what happens when those individuals come together as a self-organizing team. Motivation without freedom can wither; freedom without motivation can flounder. But when trust meets self-organization, the results are transformative.

For organizations, the message is clear. Leaders and stakeholders play a critical role in setting vision, providing support, and ensuring alignment with business goals. But the moment they cross the line into micromanagement, they choke off the very creativity and problem-solving ability they hired their teams for. Just like Jacob had to learn, leaders must step back to let teams step up. And just like Kabir's father demonstrated, when trust is given, teams don't just manage – they flourish and even scale into new territories.

The consequences of ignoring this are costly. Micromanagement leads to turnover, burnout, and wasted potential. Teams stop thinking for themselves because they know their ideas won't see the light of day. On the other hand, the benefits of embracing this principle are enormous. Teams that self-organize are more resilient, more innovative, and more capable of delivering solutions that leadership alone could never design.

By reinforcing Chapter 5 here in Chapter 11, I want you as the reader to see the bigger picture: Agile is not a set of isolated principles. It is an interconnected mindset where one principle builds on another. Trusting motivated individuals (Principle 5) is the seed. Self-organization (Principle 11) is the tree that grows from it. Together, they create an environment where the best architectures, requirements, and designs can emerge – whether in a software team, a grocery store, or a global organization.

And here's why this metaphor matters: it's not just poetic, it's practical. Without trust, the seed never takes root, and self-organization can't grow. Without self-organization, trust never multiplies beyond the individual.

One without the other is incomplete – but together, they create living systems that thrive.

This happens everywhere and not just in the grocery store. Agile is in plain sight. We just have to look closely. In this chapter, words like architecture, requirement, and design might sound like technical jargon, reserved for software developers or engineers. But if we look around, we realize these concepts play out in everyday life – and often in ways more powerful than in the workplace. One of the benefits of this book is to demystify those terms and show their true meaning in relatable ways, so that you, the reader, can see Agile not as a methodology locked inside IT departments, but as a way of thinking that applies to life itself.

Take, for example, the environment of an emergency room. When multiple patients come in after a major accident, the doctors, nurses, and specialists don't stop to wait for written requirements or a top-down design of who should do what. There is no whiteboard diagram laid out in advance with arrows pointing to everyone's role. Instead, the team self-organizes. One doctor begins stabilizing a patient, another prepares for surgery, a nurse sets up IVs, and others coordinate with technicians and family members. Each step flows into the next, guided not by a rigid script but by training, trust, and the shared goal of saving lives. That's architecture, requirements, and design unfolding in real time – not on paper, but in practice.

What makes this even more powerful is that it happens seamlessly. No single person dictates the entire process. Of course, leadership and expertise are present – the ER chief or lead surgeon is like the father in the grocery store, setting direction and providing support – but the execution comes from the team's ability to self-organize in the moment. The best design for handling the crisis emerges from those on the front lines, not from a manual handed down from above.

Now pause and mirror this to your own personal or professional life. Where have you seen this kind of natural self-organization? Maybe it was at home when your family prepared for a holiday dinner. No one handed out written requirements, but somehow one person cooked, another set the table, someone else handled decorations, and everything came together. Or maybe it was at work outside of tech, when colleagues rallied around a last-minute client request and each person picked up a piece of the puzzle until the solution was ready. These examples are not limited to project management or software delivery. They are reminders that Agile principles are life principles.

And here's the key: when you start noticing these patterns, you also become better at spotting the anti-patterns. You'll recognize micromanagement when it shows up – the moment when someone insists on controlling every detail, and suddenly the energy of the group drops. You'll notice when teams stop thinking for themselves, because they've been conditioned to wait for instructions. On the other hand, you'll also recognize when the principle is alive and in flight – when people are organizing themselves, solving problems, and creating results greater than the sum of their parts.

When you can see both sides – the anti-patterns and the healthy patterns – you're in a stronger position to respond. You can step in, like I did in Chapter 5 with Jacob's team, and help mitigate micromanagement by empowering the group. Or you can choose to be more like Kabir's father, who modeled trust by stepping back and letting his children thrive. Both perspectives reinforce the lesson that self-organization doesn't mean absence of leadership, but rather the presence of trust, support, and freedom to act.

Agile Principle #11 is not just a statement about software. It's a statement about human potential. Whether in a grocery store, an emergency room, a holiday gathering, or a corporate project, the best architectures, requirements, and designs emerge not from strict control, but from people working together, organizing themselves, and responding to the reality in front of them. Once you start looking closely, you'll see it everywhere.

And if you remember nothing else from this chapter, remember this: Principle 5 plants the seed, and Principle 11 grows it into a tree. One gives life, the other gives strength – together, they create the conditions where teams, families, and organizations can truly thrive.

Takeaway for Readers:
The best architectures, requirements, and designs emerge from self-organizing teams.

The best leaders don't pull the strings tighter – they loosen them. Kabir's father didn't lose control by stepping back; he gained something far more valuable: children who could run and even scale the business without him. In organizations, the same is true. When leaders trust teams to self-organize, they don't diminish their role; they multiply their impact.

Self-organization is not about chaos or lack of control – it's about structured trust. Just like Kabir and his siblings took ownership of the grocery store without a rulebook, teams thrive when leaders step back and allow them to shape their own approach. The best results often come not from strict instructions but from people closest to the work making the right decisions in the moment.

Freedom without responsibility can lead to failure, but freedom with responsibility creates sustainable results. Kabir wasn't just given a store; he was trusted to manage it, make decisions, and oversee staff. In the same way, when teams are empowered with accountability, they deliver outcomes far greater than what a rulebook could produce.

Chapter 12

Reflection in Motion: The Power of Looking Back to Move Forward

This chapter might just be the most valuable one in this entire book – not because it's the most detailed, but because it speaks to something deeply human: the need to reflect. Whether you're navigating the chaos of a fast-paced project or wrestling with personal challenges, the ability to pause, reflect, and learn from your journey is what truly fuels growth.

In Agile, one of the ceremonies I've grown to deeply appreciate is the retrospective. It's a moment when the team comes together – not to plan forward, but to reflect backward. What went well? What didn't? And most importantly – what can we improve? This simple yet powerful ritual doesn't just apply to product development; it's a life tool.

That's exactly what Agile Principle #12 reminds us of:

"At regular intervals, the team reflects on how to become more effective, then tunes and adjusts its behavior accordingly."

This principle is more than a guideline for software teams – it's a powerful reminder that intentional reflection is key to continuous growth in any part of life.

I've often wondered – why did they place this as principle number twelve? Why not number one, or two, or smack in the middle at eight? It's almost like the Agile Manifesto saved the best for last. Think about it – after emphasizing things like working software, customer collaboration, face-to-face communication, and self-organization, it ends with a gentle but powerful nudge: "Don't forget to look back." That's no coincidence.

For example, in Scrum – one of the most popular Agile frameworks – the retrospective is the final ceremony in every sprint. You plan, you build, you review – and then, you reflect. It's like the Agile universe saying, "Before you rush into the next thing, pause and ask yourself – what did we learn?" It's the dessert after a full-course delivery sprint – sweet, essential, and much needed, especially when the main course had its fair share of bugs and blockers.

This chapter will dive into the power of retrospection and why it's essential to both individual and team growth. It sets the foundation for the stories that follow – moments where reflection led to reinvention. But before we get there, let's understand why retrospection isn't just an Agile principle – it's a life principle.

By the time you finish reading the stories in this chapter, you'll come to understand that retrospection – what Agile Principle #12 points us toward – doesn't require a formal setting or structured ceremony. In fact, reflection can happen in the most ordinary moments: during a long walk, after a tough conversation, in the middle of chaos, or even while watching a movie. The point is: we don't need to wait for an official invitation to reflect.

This is why I often say, Agile is in plain sight. Its principles aren't confined to storyboards or standups – they're woven into the fabric of our everyday lives. We just need to slow down long enough to see them, name them, and apply them with intention.

Let me take you back to one of the most unforgettable football moments in recent history – a moment that became a metaphor for Agile thinking in my own journey.

Football – known as soccer in the United States – is more than just a game in many parts of the world. In Europe, it's a cultural pillar, a weekly ritual, and a source of identity for millions. And at the pinnacle of European club football sits the UEFA Champions League – a tournament that brings together the best teams from across various countries in Europe to battle it out for one of the most coveted trophies in the sport.

The Champions League isn't just about winning; it's about legacy. Each match carries immense pressure, pride, and the hopes of fans around the globe. To win this tournament is to etch your name in history – so every step in the journey matters.

The UEFA Champions League began in 1955, originally called the European Champion Clubs' Cup. The first club to win it was Real Madrid, who went on to dominate the early years, winning five consecutive titles from 1956 to 1960. The tournament evolved into its current format in 1992, increasing both its competitiveness and global appeal.

Over the decades, the Champions League has become a stage for legendary clubs. Teams like Real Madrid, FC Barcelona, AC Milan, Chelsea, Liverpool, Manchester United, Bayern Munich, and Juventus have not only graced the tournament but have shaped its narrative. Their rivalries, comebacks, heartbreaks, and triumphs are the lifeblood of what makes the competition so compelling.

So, reaching the final means you've already conquered giants and endured intense competition. The Champions League isn't a straight road; it's a gauntlet of high-stakes knockout rounds, where one poor night can erase months of hard work. Every goal counts. Every away match tests your resilience, tactics, and mental strength.

So when two legendary clubs like Liverpool and Barcelona meet in the semifinals – a two-legged showdown that decides who advances to the final – the world must stop to watch. Not just because of the names involved, but because of what's at stake: a shot at football immortality.

In the first leg of the 2019 UEFA Champions League semifinal, Liverpool faced Barcelona at the Camp Nou in Spain, the home ground of Barcelona football club. Despite putting in a solid performance and creating several clear chances, Liverpool walked away with nothing to show for it. They hit the post, forced key saves from the Barcelona keeper, and pushed forward with intensity – but were ultimately punished by clinical finishing from the likes of Luis Suárez and Lionel Messi.

The scoreboard read 3–0 in favor of Barcelona. On paper, it looked like a rout. But anyone who watched that match knew the story was more layered than the result suggested. Liverpool didn't lack effort – they lacked outcome.

Fast forward six days later to Anfield – Liverpool FC's iconic home ground. The atmosphere was electric, though slightly somber without star forwards Mohamed Salah and Roberto Firmino, both ruled out due to injury.

From the first whistle, Liverpool pressed high, played with purpose, and exposed Barcelona's vulnerabilities. The energy was different – sharper, smarter, more adaptive. Just seven minutes in, Liverpool scored their first goal, igniting hope across the stadium.

But football is nothing if not unpredictable. As if things weren't already tough for Liverpool, left-back Andy Robertson picked up an injury in the first half and had to be replaced. In came Georginio Wijnaldum, who hadn't even made the starting lineup.

Then, everything changed.

Wijnaldum scored twice in quick succession, leveling the aggregate to 3–3. A substitution turned game-changer.

And then came the 79th minute – a moment of sheer brilliance. With Barcelona's defense caught off guard, Trent Alexander-Arnold whipped in a cheeky, quick corner to Divock Origi, who slotted home the decisive fourth goal.

Chaos. Genius. Adaptation in real time.

With that result against Barcelona, an aggregate score of 4–3 – Liverpool advanced to the final of the 2019 UEFA Champions League, completing one of the greatest comebacks in football history. In the final, they faced their Premier League counterpart, Tottenham Hotspur, and secured a 2–0 victory to lift the trophy.

The final match was held at the Wanda Metropolitano Stadium in Madrid, Spain – a fitting stage for a team that had demonstrated resilience, reflection, and relentless adaptability every step of the way.

Going back to that semifinal game – as I sat there after the match, still buzzing from what I'd just witnessed – I couldn't shake the feeling that I had seen something bigger than football. It wasn't just the goals or the comeback. It was how Liverpool carried themselves, how they responded after a tough first leg, and how every player showed up with renewed energy and belief.

The second leg wasn't just a game – it felt like a response, a statement.

Take the substitution of Andy Robertson, for example. His injury wasn't part of the plan. But Liverpool's response – bringing in Georginio Wijnaldum, who hadn't even started – was a masterclass in agility. They didn't panic or stick rigidly to a preset formation. They adapted in real time. Wijnaldum's unexpected entry and immediate impact was like a mid-sprint pivot: unplanned, but critical to success.

In Agile terms, it was as if the team identified a blocker mid-sprint, adjusted their backlog priorities on the fly, and deployed the perfect feature right when it mattered most. That substitution became the turning point – not because it was pre-designed, but because the team had built a culture ready to adjust when circumstances changed.

Even though I barely had time to celebrate or text my friends before jumping into a Sprint Review meeting, the match lingered in my mind. It gave me clarity – a real-life example of resilience, adaptation, team trust, and how timely adjustments can turn everything around.

For context, the match was played during the afternoon hours in the United States – around 12 PM to 2 PM Pacific Time – which aligned perfectly with my lunch break. In Europe, where the game took place, it was evening, under the lights at Anfield. That time zone difference somehow deepened the moment for me: while Europe was preparing to wind down, I was in the middle of my workday, switching gears from one kind of team performance to another.

The passion, adaptability, and energy I had just witnessed on the pitch stayed with me as I entered the Sprint Review meeting 30 minutes later.

As people began joining the call, a few business leads trickled in late from their earlier meetings. As the Agile Lead, I've always believed in using lighthearted icebreakers to set the right tone before diving into the agenda.

With the excitement still fresh in me, my team – knowing I'm a die-hard Liverpool fan – seized the perfect opportunity and kicked things off with a smile:

"Adewale, how was the game?"

I couldn't help but grin.

"Unbelievable," I said. "That wasn't just football – it was a masterclass in grit and adaptation. No Salah, no Firmino, but we still found a way."

I gave a quick, animated recap of the goals, especially that clever corner from Alexander-Arnold. My energy was contagious. A few of the business leads who had either watched the game or seen the final score on their phones jumped in too – laughing, shaking their heads in disbelief, and tossing in their own reactions.

"*That fourth goal was genius,*" one of them said.

Another admitted, *"I only saw the highlights, but man... what a comeback."*

For a few minutes, the meeting transformed into a casual huddle – a space of shared excitement and connection before we shifted into Sprint Review mode.

It was after the Sprint Review meeting that something clicked for me.

I found myself thinking, wait a minute… that match we casually discussed as an icebreaker at the start of the Sprint Review was actually a live retrospective. In the moment, I was simply riding the emotional high of the win. The conversation felt like a lighthearted pre-meeting moment.

But looking back, I realized that what Jürgen Klopp the Liverpool FC coach and his team did between those two matches embodied everything about Agile retrospectives.

They reflected.

They adjusted.

They delivered differently.

And just like that, what started as a simple post-lunch, icebreaker conversation became a powerful eye-opener – reminding me that retrospectives aren't always about formal techniques, sticky notes, or whiteboards. It's about the action we choose to take in order to get better – whether we're prepared or not. It's a mindset.

So, I started thinking about how I could bring this moment into our next retrospective – not just as a storytelling exercise, but as a source of motivation.

The connection was too powerful to ignore.

Klopp's team didn't just show resilience; they modeled exactly what we in Agile strive for every sprint: awareness, adaptation, and improvement.

I thought, what if this story could help us see retrospectives differently – not as a checkbox at the end of a sprint, but as a real chance to transform how we work together?

But then reality kicked in.

I looked at my team and realized: not everyone knows Liverpool Football Club. And even if they do, not everyone follows soccer. Some might not care at all about the Champions League or dramatic comebacks at Anfield.

So I paused and asked myself, How do I make this relatable without losing the essence of what I'm trying to share?

That's when the bigger idea hit me:

This isn't just a soccer story – it's a sports story.

And sports, in some form, connect with almost everyone. Whether it's basketball, tennis, Formula 1, or track and field, every sport has one thing in common: the pursuit of improvement.

Teams and athletes constantly watch replays, analyze their performance, and make adjustments – not because they failed, but because they want to grow stronger, faster, and smarter.

That's retrospection in its purest form.

So, I decided: yes, I'll share the Liverpool story. But I'll frame it in a way that speaks to a broader truth across all sports and teams – every great team reflects.

Every winning mindset pauses to ask, how can we be better than we were yesterday?

And if they can do it in stadiums and locker rooms, then surely, we can do it in our sprint rooms and Zoom calls.

After all, the drive to become better than before isn't just a sports ambition – it's a human one.

If we take a closer look at the game – both legs – it becomes clear: this wasn't just a football comeback. It was Agile in motion. And this isn't just a football story – it's an Agile story.

After a crushing 3–0 defeat at Camp Nou in the first leg, Klopp and his coaching team didn't just blame luck or individual mistakes. They treated the loss like a sprint retrospective.

What worked? What didn't? What could be improved?

Liverpool recognized where Barcelona exploited space and controlled the tempo, and how their own attacking rhythm was stifled. They reviewed footage, gathered player feedback, reflected without ego, and crafted an action plan rooted in evidence and intent.

But just like in Agile, it wasn't the analysis that mattered – it was what they did with it.

This wasn't theoretical analysis for its own sake – it was the practical execution of insights. Agile retrospectives are only as powerful as the decisions they influence. Liverpool made bold changes based on learning: new players, higher pressing, and smarter transitions.

Even the now-iconic quick corner kick that led to the decisive goal wasn't a scripted play or a rigid plan. It was the result of a team empowered to adapt in the moment – a blend of awareness, fast thinking, and the freedom to experiment.

That's Agile in action.

What surprised me most was how this conversation began to ripple through my team. It didn't stay a story – it became a shift in mindset.

During our next retrospective, I shared the story of the game – just as I had planned – and the energy in the room was different. Team members started to truly understand what it means to embrace change, to stay ready for change, and to approach challenges with the goal of becoming better – not just getting things done.

Some even brought their own perspectives to the table. One person related it to basketball, another to baseball, and someone else drew parallels from American football – highlighting how every great team, no matter the sport, constantly adjusts, reviews tape, and adapts to what's next.

But what really struck me was when one team member used an emergency room team as a case study. They explained how doctors, nurses, and specialists have to regroup quickly after every critical moment – evaluating what worked, what didn't, and how to improve in real time to save lives. Another team member shared an everyday example: driving on freeways, adjusting to speed limits that vary between counties. They emphasized how awareness and adaptability keep us moving safely and effectively – just like in Agile.

Some even went on YouTube to rewatch the highlights of both legs of the match, seeing with fresh eyes what resilience, reflection, and adaptation actually look like in motion.

That's when I knew the message had landed. Using the Champions League showdown between Liverpool and Barcelona, along with other sports and real-life analogies, helped unlock something powerful. My team didn't just hear the concept of retrospection – they started to live it.

So, retrospection isn't about looking back for the sake of nostalgia or blame. It's about learning with clarity, adjusting with courage, and trusting the team enough to execute change.

Agile isn't just a framework – it's a mindset. And sometimes, you don't see it in a sprint planning session or a Scrum board. Sometimes, you see it in the electric atmosphere of Anfield – or in the quiet, everyday moments of life, if we just pay close enough attention.

Takeaway for Readers:
At regular intervals, the team reflects on how to become more effective, then tunes and adjusts its behavior accordingly.

Agile teams must not fear failure – they must face it openly. Retrospectives aren't just meetings at the end of a sprint; they are a mindset. The real value lies not in pointing fingers or assigning blame, but in pulling insights from experience and acting on them with intention. It's the courage to reflect – and act on that reflection – that turns failure into transformation. Reflection, when done with honesty and bravery, becomes a launchpad for growth. Learning only matters when it leads to meaningful change.

More importantly, retrospection isn't limited to the end of a sprint. The best Agile teams know how to adapt in real time, shifting direction mid-sprint when circumstances demand it. Whether on a football pitch, in a hospital emergency room, or navigating changing freeway speed limits, agility lives in the ability to respond – quickly, intentionally, and together. The ability to pause, reflect, and adjust isn't just good practice; it's what turns teams into high-performing team, and moments into momentum.

Acknowledgments

I am grateful to my family and friends for their love, support, patience, and constant encouragement throughout the journey of writing this book. A special appreciation to my late grandmother, Olanike Ejide Adetokun, who raised me and instilled in me the values that shaped me into a strategic thinker and a great storyteller. Her influence continues to guide my path.

Growing up in Nigeria molded my character in ways I continue to cherish, teaching me resilience, discipline, humility, and the courage to dream beyond my environment. Those early lessons carried me across oceans. My journey in the United States strengthened those same values and opened doors to new perspectives, opportunities, and experiences. Together, both worlds shaped not just my life, but my voice, my leadership, and the purpose behind this book.

Special thanks to Lanre "eLDee" Dabiri. Thank you for your guidance, your wisdom, and for helping me grow into the Agile practitioner I am today.

To the teams I've had the privilege to work with over the years, your collaboration, challenges, breakthroughs, and shared experiences inspired many of the stories in this book. I'm grateful for every lesson and every moment that pushed me to grow.

My sincere appreciation goes to my editor, Chirota "Chi Ohi" Akhazemea, for bringing clarity, structure, and strength to this project. You helped turn my thoughts into something I can be proud of.

And finally, to you - the reader. Thank you for choosing this book and welcoming my voice into your journey. I hope these insights empower you, challenge you, and inspire your own growth in the Agile world and beyond.